The God Touch

Dr. Gene Lingerfelt

The God Touch

ISBN: 0-9770398-1-1

Published by

LifeBridge
Books
P.O. BOX 49428
CHARLOTTE, NC 28277

Printed in the United States of America.

Dedication

*To my bride, my love and
my inspiration, Suzanne Marie.*

CONTENTS

FOREWORD

I have shared the good news about Jesus Christ with millions of people in over eighty nations. I have observed the religions of the world. They can be very confusing. Even the Christian religion is often made to seem abstract and bewildering.

My friend, the author of this powerful book is practical. He believes God wants to be your friend, that He cares about you and He believes in you so much He paid an enormous price to remove the barrier of sin which has separated you from Him.

The obstruction of your sins was eliminated when Jesus assumed your guilt and endured your judgment in His death on the cross. That is the big fact of your redemption. Your sins have been paid for. God holds nothing against you and He wants to be a part of *every area* of your life. Maybe you, like millions of others, haven't realized that.

This book will show you the facts of this good news. When you believe these truths and decide in your heart to embrace Christ as your Savior *and* Friend, He will come to you while you read, and will begin to live IN YOU because the fact is your sins have already been expunged through His death on the cross. When He died, He paid your penalty. Now, nothing stands between you and Him.

Read these pages with a "Yes!" in your heart. *Believe* and *embrace* each simple truth, step by step, and you will discover *peace with God through your Lord Jesus Christ* and *life abundantly* (Romans 5:1; John 10:10).

You are created by LOVE. God is love. This book will lead you right into the loving presence of our Lord. You will be confident in your relationship with Him because you will understand how and why your salvation is a living reality—in *every part* of your life.

Friendship with God is not a matter of trying to be holy or "churchy" or super-spiritual. It is based on understanding how God regards you, why He loves you, how much He believes in you, the price He has already paid—and how He wants your friendship more than you ever desired His.

Read this beautiful book and welcome the presence, the life, the love and the friendship of God as you discover the exhilarating fact that before you finish these chapters, YOU will have *The God Touch* upon YOUR life.

– Dr. T. L. Osborn

PART ONE

WALKING IN FINANCIAL COVENANT WITH GOD MOST HIGH

Chapter One

Abraham – The Covenant Man

I want to tell you about a place too few people ever become acquainted with. Most individuals today live out their entire lives with a sense of loneliness—a feeling of being totally on their own. But there is a place where each individual can walk and talk with God, counting on Him just as Adam did back in the garden.

Let me share with you the secret of *"Walking In Financial Covenant With God Most High."*

There is a place where you can:

- Lose all fear of man.
- Know all things are working for your good.
- Know that whatever you put your hand to will prosper.
- Know you cannot fail.
- Know you will forever be moving forward financially, not regressing backwards.
- Know that God is your source, not man.

A "Confession"

Right here, in the midst of our time together, I want you to repeat a "confession." Even now—while you're reading this book—say these words out loud: "I'm not a moocher. I am a producer! I'm not a beggar. I am a dominion taker! Whatever I put my hands to prospers. It is the will of God that I succeed in this life. God has a plan for me, so I am going to work His divine plan and prosper more than ever before."

God Spoke

In Genesis chapter 12, God spoke to a man named Abraham, and called him out in a day when there was not any written Word. That's hard for us to understand. Moses—who wrote more of the Old Testament than any other writer—had not yet been born.

God revealed Himself to Abraham living in ancient Babylonia—modern day Iraq—and called him to leave his home, family, property and inheritance. The Lord was saying, *"Come, follow and walk in covenant with Me."*

It's truly astounding. With no written revelation, Abraham answered the call and began on his journey. His only initial mistake was taking a relative with him, a man named Lot. However, even though Abraham obeyed God, from the time he left home with Lot until they departed ways, the Almighty never spoke to Abraham. In order to walk in financial covenant with God Most High, there had to be a separation from Abraham's old ways of doing things— a detachment from his previous connections.

The Identification

As the Bible records, Abraham identified himself with God and

Lot aligned himself with a town called Sodom. (Later we find out that God destroyed Sodom and Gomorrah because they had associated themselves with a so-called "alternate lifestyle" of homosexuality.)

In Genesis 14, we read of a war between nine kings—four on one side, five on the other. The four kings had been receiving financial tribute from the lesser five kings, and it wasn't long before the five rebelled and initiated the battle (Genesis 14:9). One of the five kings happened to be the king of Sodom.

Scripture describes how this king and his allies lost the battle and in the process of this loss, Abraham's nephew, Lot, was taken captive. Why? Because he had improperly aligned himself. In today's language we would say, "He was in the wrong place at the wrong time."

While Abraham had chosen the high country, Lot pitched his tents toward Sodom—and now we find him actually living there.

The Right Choice

As a pastor, I pray people will understand the consequences of aligning themselves with negative forces—since it can end in tragedy.

In the modern daytime talk shows, people are incessantly excuse-making, saying, "Well, one thing led to another." That is an excuse, but it is also true. One bad decision can lead to the next, and ultimately to disaster.

This was the case in Lot's life. He pitched his tents *toward* Sodom, then, before long, began living *in* Sodom. Because of his alignment with this wicked city and it's "alternative lifestyle," when Sodom fell, Lot and his family were taken hostage.

This is plainly seen in the text of Genesis 14:11-12: *"The four kings seized all the goods of Sodom and Gomorrah and all their food; then they went away. They also carried off Abraham's nephew Lot and his possessions, since..."* Notice the Bible specifically says "since." *"...since he was living in Sodom."* Therefore, if Lot had not been residing there, the situation would never have occurred.

He Rose Up

Abraham—without a second thought—gathered together 318 men who were in his employ and trained in warfare (Genesis 14:16). Think of Abraham's wealth. You have to be a man of financial means to hire such a huge number of skilled men as employees— not counting the untrained men, women and children. This army defeated the four kings who had attacked Sodom and also kidnaped his nephew Lot—plus Lot's family! Think about it: four kings rise up against five kings and they defeat the majority. But Abraham goes out to battle and conquers these same four victorious kings.

Scripture tells us *"[Abraham] recovered all the goods and brought back his relative Lot and his possessions, together with the women and the other people"* (Genesis14:16) The story continues: *"Then Melchizedek king of Salem brought out bread and wine. He was priest of God Most High, and he blessed Abraham, saying, 'Blessed be Abraham by God Most High, Creator of heaven and earth. And blessed be God Most High, who delivered your enemies into your hand.' Then Abram gave him a tenth of everything. The king of Sodom said to Abraham, 'Give me the people and keep the goods for yourself.' But Abraham said to the king of Sodom, 'I have raised my hand to the Lord, God Most High, Creator of heaven and earth, and have taken an oath that I will accept nothing belonging to you, not even a thread or the thong of a sandal, so that you will never be able to say, 'I made Abraham rich'"* (vv.18-23).

There is a place in God where few of His people ever dwell. I am talking about a "zone," if you will, where you can "walk in covenant with God." And one aspect of this blessed dwelling place is walking in *financial* covenant.

Many believers never discover what this means and spend their entire lives living paycheck to paycheck. As a result, each generation of God's people must essentially start over from scratch because their godly, church-going parents weren't able to leave them an inheritance.

Abraham learned how to walk in financial covenant with God before there was even a written revelation of the Almighty. Yet, here we are today, approximately five thousand years later, with 66 books of the Bible available for us to study, meditate upon and renew our minds, yet we still have believers struggling with this concept of walking in the blessings of God.

The Nature Of Authority

Years ago I wrote a study course I called *"Spiritual Authority"* for the members of our church. At the time, I admit I didn't actually *understand* all the principles I had discovered in the Word of God. I just assumed they were true and all worked because I had indeed found them in Scripture.

On the other hand, many are *waiting* to understand the Bible before they will act on it. This is not necessary. For example, you don't understand gravity, but you depend on it every day. Each time you turn on a food blender you may not understand the principles of physics behind centrifugal force, yet you employ them on your behalf.

Consider Moses. How many times did the children of Israel rise up to unfairly criticize, backbite and complain against him? Yet, he never took it personally, and was able to understand they were only hurting themselves. By their grumbling and murmuring, the children of Israel were not harming Moses. In fact, on one occasion God said to him,

"Stand aside and let me put an end to them at once and I will make a great nation out of you" (Exodus 32:10).

Walking In Covenant With God

How was Moses able to accomplish such great things? Because he was walking as Abraham walked: in covenant with God. Moses understood he was a *covenant man*. It was not the children of Israel who had the revelation at the burning bush and the *people* were not the ones who held the staff in their hand. So whatever the children of Israel did was *their* problem—and only limiting themselves.

This is also why Melchizedek came out to greet and bless Abraham. Some might ask, "Where was Melchizedek when all of the fighting was going on? And how is it he showed up *after* the battle—as a priest, a representative of God Most High—and received a tithe from Abraham?"

Melchizedek serves a twofold purpose: to be a true representative of God to remind Abraham, "You are blessed!"

Today, those called by God to minister have the same two functions. First, to make *you* mindful that you have not accomplished what you have by your education or your "smarts," but you have only come this far because of the favor of God on your life. This is important since whenever we begin thinking it is by our intellect, or because we were born in America, or happen to be of a certain race, we set ourselves up for failure.

Second, it is to remind us we are blessed of God.

A Tenth Of Everything

The Bible tells us, *"...Abram gave him a tenth of everything"* (Genesis 14:20).

Why would Abraham do this—especially without a written

revelation or record of God's will regarding tithing? Remember, Abel did the same. Cain brought *some* fruits to God, but Abel somehow had a revelation to bring *first* fruits to the Creator. This is exactly what the tithe is; a "first fruit" unto God.

A tithe is a recognition, an acknowledgment, that I have done what I have done, I have produced what I have produced, by the grace and by the provision of God Most High—and that in turn makes me God's debtor. I have reaped a harvest of fruit, or livestock, or money from His earth, and I owe Him a tenth. I am making my living off of His good graces, therefore I owe Him what He requires.

To add more clarity regarding the tithe, *"The king of Sodom said to Abraham, 'Give me the people and keep the goods for yourself.' But Abraham said to the king of Sodom, 'I have raised my hand to the Lord, God Most High, Creator of heaven and earth, and have taken an oath that I will accept nothing belonging to you, not even a thread or the thong of a sandal, so that you will never be able to say, "I made Abraham rich"'"* (vv.21-32).

This is the heart of the concept of "walking in *financial* covenant with God Most High." Abraham had an understanding that he was *independently* in financial covenant with Jehovah.

The operative word is "independently," because as long as you see your prosperity level as being relative to anything, then you are not walking as Abraham did. If you perceive your abundance as being related to our Federal Reserve Chairman, the stock market, the unemployment rate, or to what the government is doing to you or for you, then you are not walking as God desires.

Evaluate Yourself

Abraham acted in boldness and without worry or fear of failure, because he saw himself in this covenant. Since this was Abraham's self-image, it allowed him to be free of others. It really did not matter if the four kings came against him, or if the king of Sodom wanted to offer him a gift. These actions had nothing to do with Abraham because he was not dependent on the king of Sodom or anyone else. Abraham was not walking in partnership with an earthly king—but in covenant with Almighty God.

He was not afraid to go to war. Why? Because before he even entered into battle, Abraham already knew what the outcome would be. He knew it was impossible for him to put his hand to something and fail, or to have less this year than he had last year. Abraham understood he was independently walking in financial covenant with God Most High. This is why he was able to boldly say to the king of Sodom, *"... I will accept nothing belonging to you, not even a thread or the thong of a sandal, so that you will never be able to say, 'I made Abraham rich'"* (v.23).

I remember the time a man was personally upset with me. He made up his mind to do everything possible to malign me and bring disgrace numerically and financially in our ministry. But I never uttered a word or lashed out. Why? Because the Lord spoke three things into my heart. First, as to the people who were aligning themselves with him, the Lord said, "Don't count them."

Why would God emphasize that point? Because as long as you are counting what you have lost, you are not focused on what you have—or have coming. Also, in God's Work, you can only minister to people who are *present.*

Evaluate The Circumstances

The second thing the Lord spoke into my heart was, "What does this have to do with you?" I meditated on Moses and how no matter what the children of Israel did to him or accused him of, Moses never retaliated. Why? Because he understood—just as Abraham did—that he was independently walking in covenant with God Most High. So, what other people did to (or said about) Moses didn't matter at all. Only what God declared concerning Moses was important—and what the leader was saying about himself and doing during his testing at the hands of men.

"That Has Nothing To Do With You"

The third instruction the Lord gave me was, "That has *nothing* to do with you." Immediately, I understood what God had said to Moses and Abraham.

In the course of this incident, if thoughts of what the man was doing to oppose me came to my mind, I would say out loud, "That has nothing to do with me." I even spoke those words in public—in a restaurant, a staff meeting, and in some of my sermons. Every time I was tempted to grieve or be anxious concerning the matter, I would declare those words aloud.

As long as you perceive the little clique that doesn't like you on the job has something to do with your prosperity level, then they do indeed. The same is true if you believe some unknown group of people is out to get you, or you think your boss is holding you back, Why? Because that is your perception—and your beliefs either release or limit your faith and actions.

Walking The Earth As A Covenant Person

Since Abraham gave God the "first fruits" of all that crossed his hand, he was not walking the earth as other men did. Rather, he was a covenant man! And something more: Abraham realized people cannot successfully put their hands on, diminish or hold a covenant man down.

Even though the individual I referred to earlier did everything in his power to damage our ministry, the very next year our attendance increased by nineteen percent—even more because we had to replace those who had left the fellowship because of this man. However, since we were walking independently in covenant with God, what he did or said had nothing to do with us.

Likewise, the devil's antics will not affect you. Even if you are laid off from you job, the Lord has something much better in store.

You have two choices: you can walk in covenant or you can whine and cry. Whether you are white, black or Hispanic, you have no reason to complain because as a child of God you have every advantage.

Some time ago, when I was preaching the Gospel overseas, a minister called my home to tell my wife he could not pay his bills—and wanted me to help him.

Those who do not walk in financial covenant with God—even if they are ministers, will always turn to those who do. Why? Because they do not understand God's laws of abundance.

You Must Be A Tither

There are two kinds of Christians—tithers and "seed corn eaters." The second group has no business judging a covenant man.

When non-tithers criticize tithers, they are begging.

As a Christian you are now a part of the kingdom of God and have entered into the household of faith. Church should never become the Jerry Springer Show—where we expose our sad tales in an attempt to gain sympathy.

No, we are prevailing, overcoming and taking dominion over our world by the mighty Word of our God. We do not trod the earth as other men and women do; we are in covenant with the Almighty. We are giving Him the first fruits of all that crosses our hands, and nothing—*no weapon formed against us*—shall prosper or prevail (Isaiah 54:17). It is impossible for us to go into battle and fail. Say it out loud, "I do not walk the earth as others do."

Abraham had such a reality because he not only *had* faith, he acted on it!

When I was five years old, my mother regularly took me to Bethesda Missionary Temple in Detroit, Michigan. In Sunday School they told me about Jesus and I gave my life to Him and asked Him to be my Lord.

Almost immediately, they handed me a tithing envelope and taught how God says we are to give one penny out of every ten to His work. I began consistently giving the Lord what belongs to Him and have never stopped. For more than 40 years I have lived on ten percent less.

The world is also filled with people who are eating their seed corn—every week, every month, every year. They vacation, buy clothes and purchase an extra car on God's tithes—enjoying what I was doing without. Then, when God began to bless me abundantly, the non-tithers began to complain.

I've heard people moan, "Somebody did me wrong," or "I've been held back." They don't deserve a hand-out, instead they need to act on the Word of God and enter into a financial covenant with the Father.

With God You're Not Inadequate

If you are fired from your job, it is not a sign of your deficiency or

God's inability. I smiled when I told my congregation, "I've been laid off twice in my life, and neither company is still in business today. It was not a testament to my inadequacy, but a demonstration of their stupidity!"

What man meant for harm, God meant for good. Since I was walking independently in financial covenant with the Father, it wasn't really man who laid me off. No, it was God gently pushing me out of the nest. In those days I was content just showing up for work and cashing my meager paycheck. The Lord used the experience to prod me and say, "It's time to dust off your resume—time to advance."

When Abraham learned his nephew had been taken captive, he could easily have fallen apart and cried, "But Lord, I obeyed you. I came from Ur of the Chaldeans. And since then nothing has gone right in my life." He could have asked someone for counseling. However, since Abraham understood he was in covenant with Almighty God, he went out and reclaimed not only what was his, but even more. Then he gave God a tithe of *all.*

Abraham presented the Lord with the "first fruit" of what had been delivered into his hands via a wealth transfer of the wicked unto the righteous.

As we will discover, this was the start of a mighty partnership.

Chapter Two

Abraham's Power of Partnership

During a recent flight to Africa, the Lord asked me, "How long has it been since you taught on tithing?" Trying to jog my memory, I replied, "I have no idea."

"Well, now is the time!" God told me.

Upon our arrival home from the missions trip, we began looking for additional land with expressway frontage for the expansion and relocation of our ministry. Have you ever gone shopping and had in mind exactly what you wanted to buy? Whether you plan to purchase a suit or an automobile, the price is always more than you anticipate. It was also true with the land we were interested in.

During those days I also began to meditate on Genesis 14—the story we discussed in Chapter 1—where Abraham gave his tithe to Melchizedek, priest of God Most High. As I began to teach at our church on God's financial blessings through tithing I thought about the upcoming expensive purchase of property and told the congregation,

"I don't have time to feed you with an eyedropper like you would a bird that has just hatched out of the egg. I've got to help you become wealthy fast!"

I realized the funds for expansion would not come from sinners, but from born again believers.

The Lord Blesses His People

God finances His own kingdom—and He accomplishes this by blessing His people.

Since 1973 when I began proclaiming the Gospel, I have never once preached on giving to God sacrificially. Instead, my message has been that we give out of our abundance.

I am fully aware there are many pastors who have taught God's people they should do without—and those same ministers have to live with the results of their teaching. On the other hand, I have successfully instructed that God's people ought to live in abundance—so I am living with the fruit of my teaching.

Standing firmly on God's Word, we are unapologetic in creating an atmosphere for blessings. Why? Because it is the will of God for you to succeed in this life.

Prosperity is a misunderstood theme, yet it gives those around us a testimony of how good and great our God truly is—and what He has been accomplishing in our lives.

Labor, Connection And Partnership

Looking closely at the covenant relationship between Abraham and the Lord's representative, Melchizedek, there are three important aspects:

The first is *labor*. After reading Genesis 14, you might ask, "Why would Melchizedek receive or collect a tithe from Abraham when he wasn't even in the raiding party. Where was the labor which produced the income?"

The Bible records that part of Abraham's labor was digging water wells. He also had flocks and herds and was in the business of shepherding. And Scripture specifically states Abraham's son Isaac sowed seed for crops and reaped a hundred-fold return. That's labor!

On this occasion, Abraham went to war to rescue his nephew, Lot. In the process, the Word tells us, *"He recovered all the goods..."* (Genesis 14:16). How much? *All! "...He recovered all the goods and brought back his relative Lot and his possessions, together with the women and the other people."*

This time there was a different kind of labor—warfare. And it resulted in a supernatural harvest. This was a *wealth transfer* for Abraham because through his endeavor of warfare, he was able to acquire what had been the result of the hard work of others, the bounty which had been taken out of Sodom. In addition, Abraham also acquired the goods the four kings had with them when they went to war against Sodom and Gomorrah.

Some have heard preaching on "wealth transfers" and expect it to happen every week. However, life doesn't work that way. We go to our jobs Monday through Friday and receive the benefits of our efforts. This may continue for several years, then all of a sudden there comes a supernatural blessing of God—a wealth transfer!

This is when Deuteronomy 28 kicks into gear and we are

overtaken by the Lord's goodness. By entering into a covenant with God, here is what we can expect: *"If you fully obey the Lord your God and carefully follow all his commands I give you today, the Lord your God will set you high above all the nations on earth. All these blessings will come upon you and accompany you if you obey the Lord your God. You will be blessed in the city and blessed in the country. The fruit of your womb will be blessed, and the crops of your land and the young of your livestock—the calves of your herds and the lambs of your flocks. Your basket and your kneading trough will be blessed. You will be blessed when you come in and blessed when you go out. The Lord will grant that the enemies who rise up against you will be defeated before you. They will come at you from one direction but flee from you in seven. The Lord will send a blessing on your barns and on everything you put your hand to. The Lord your God will bless you in the land he is giving you. The Lord will establish you as his holy people, as he promised you on oath, if you keep the commands of the Lord your God and walk in his ways. Then all the peoples on earth will see that you are called by the name of the Lord, and they will fear you. The Lord will grant you abundant prosperity—in the fruit of your womb, the young of your livestock and the crops of your ground—in the land he swore to your forefathers to give you. The Lord will open the heavens, the storehouse of his bounty, to send rain on your land in season and to bless all the work of your hands. You will lend to many nations but will borrow from none. The Lord will make you the head, not the tail. If you pay attention to the commands of the Lord your God that I give you this day and carefully follow them, you will always be at the top, never at the bottom. Do not turn aside from any of the commands I give you today, to the right or to the left, following other gods and serving them"* (Deuteronomy 28:1-14).

The Word promises the blessings of God will actually "come upon" or "overtake us." The Lord's favor does not replace the necessity of labor in our lives; it is a supplement.

The Connection

I've met Christians who believe they are going to live off of divine surprises arriving in their mailbox. That's not how it happens. However, *as* we labor, *as* we do our part, every once in a while God will come along and overtake us with one of these wealth-transfer blessings.

King Solomon wrote about this: *"A good man leaves an inheritance for his children's children, but a sinner's wealth is stored up for the righteous"* (Proverbs 13:22). The King James version reads *"...the wealth of the sinner is laid up for the just."*

This obviously was never intended by God to replace hard work. Instead it is a promise intended to be an "extra" blessing, above and beyond our labor, due to the *connection* we have with God the Father.

So Abraham toiled day-to-day, but on this particular occasion, he labored through warfare. Simply stated, Abraham had the guts to step out and go into battle!

There are rewards ahead for those who are willing to take a risk.

When I was in Bible college and later in seminary, I sat in class with people who were much smarter than I was, who made better grades and probably had a higher IQ. Yet, as I have followed many of their lives, I don't see them moving into places of leadership.

I am convinced part of the blessing of God is the result of Him honoring a man or woman who receives a great vision, then steps out in faith. The Lord pours out His favor on those who march forward with boldness.

Abraham had that kind of fortitude because of his connection with Jehovah. Plus, because he was walking independently in financial covenant with the Father, he knew no fear.

As a *partner* of God, Abraham had what it took to enter into battle—knowing the Lord was with him. Because of this relationship, he was convinced he would not fail. As God's partner, fear had vanished!

It Takes Effort

Many believers are reticent to step out of the boat—to attempt anything new or different. They don't even consider sending out their resume or think of making extra income. Bound by fear, they won't venture to tell their boss they think they are qualified for a promotion. Then they come to church and wonder, "Why am I not as blessed as my neighbor who doesn't even believe in God?"

Well, if you want to see a coconut fall, you are probably going to have to shake the tree! You have got to move forward in faith—and do something tangible concerning what you say you believe. Even if you have the smallest dream, go after it!

Look at Abraham's blessing. *"Then Melchizedek king of Salem brought out bread and wine. He was priest of God Most High, and he blessed Abraham, saying, 'Blessed be Abraham by God Most High, Creator of heaven and earth. And blessed be God Most High, who delivered your enemies into your hand…'"* (Genesis 14:18-19).

It is beyond my comprehension that there are believers who still think the Lord doesn't want them to be blessed at all. Who caused

Abraham to succeed and experience a supernatural wealth transfer on that day? God did!

Walking In Covenant With God

How are you going to get God to partner His life together with yours? There is only one way: become connected to the Father.

When the Bible speaks of the blessings of the Lord, it is not referring to luck, a lottery or a matter of chance. God walks with those who *know* Him.

We make this divine connection through tithing. *"Then Abram gave him a tenth of everything"* (Genesis 14:20). Why did he do that? It could not have been because of the "law." After all, Moses had not even been born at this point, so there was no "Law of Moses" for Abraham to know and to follow.

Many modern Christians say, "Tithing is under the law and we're not under the law, so we don't tithe." However, if that is an accurate interpretation of the Bible, then why did Abraham tithe? And why did Abel give God a gift of his "first fruits"?

Tithing is a principle which both *preceded* and *succeeded* the law. In essence, giving a tenth is a law unto itself—and the scriptural foundation of prosperity.

It is also an acknowledgment that what I have produced was not by myself, but with the help and assistance of God. It is similar to when the farmer does all the labor, yet bows his head and gives his Creator thanks for the food his family is about to eat. The farmer did all the sweat work, so why should he thank God? It is because he is able to produce by his labor only because of his connection to the Father. Even if the farmer is unsaved, he is still linked to God's grace and goodness since he derives his yield from the laws of seedtime and harvest which the Almighty built into the earth at the beginning of time.

God Gives You The Power and Ability To Produce Wealth

Some may find fault and protest, "Wait a minute. God didn't plow the field, sow the seed, irrigate the land, pull the weeds and reap the harvest— the farmer did!" But the farmer would disagree, and say, "God gave me the power to do all of those things, and the Lord blesses me in the process."

Wealth is about much more than physical labor. We all know people who have worked hard their entire lives, yet they hardly have anything to show for it. If labor alone could guarantee a person's wealth, people would live in abundance all over the world.

Moses shared this principle: *"But remember the Lord your God, for it is he who gives you the ability to produce wealth, and so confirms his covenant, which he swore to your forefathers, as it is today"* (Deuteronomy 8:18). The King James version says, *"...for it is he that giveth thee power to get wealth..."* So when you give the tithe or "tenth" to God, you are doing what Moses said. Like the farmer, you are remembering and acknowledging that what you have produced is only by the grace of Almighty God.

Wealth is a matter of being blessed by God *as* you work—through labor, connection and covenant.

The Right Source

Why did Abraham give the tithe to Melchizedek? It's obvious from reading the Scripture he had a *connection* with this representative of God. He didn't just show up out of the blue and receive a tenth.

If you want your endeavors to be blessed by God, don't plug into the wrong source. For example, people who labored hard for companies such as Enron or WorldCom have not enjoyed the same level of blessing as those who worked for firms which were run more efficiently—and more honestly—by management. In the same way, if we align ourselves knowingly, or even unknowingly, with unethical or sinful behavior, there is no way we will ever reach a place of supernatural blessing in God.

I knew a man years ago who sat every Sunday in the church I pastor. And while he was connected to our ministry he owned his own home, two automobiles and enjoyed enough income his wife didn't need to work outside the home.

Without my knowledge, he became influenced by an individual in our congregation who talked him into changing his job—not a brilliant move for a man who had spent many years building his career. Nobody asked my advice, and it was really none of my business.

Not long after, the person who talked this individual into changing his job had a falling out with me due to a moral situation on his part. Subsequently, everyone he was financially connected with in the church began "moving on"—changing churches. After about a year I learned the gentleman who had switched careers was no longer living in his home; he had moved to an apartment. I soon heard his house was lost in a bank foreclosure.

As I look back on the situation, I sincerely believe that as long as that man was connected to the spiritual leadership God had provided, he was able to make enough money to support his family. But after he made this decision, he lost everything, including his marriage and family. My friend, your connections will, in large part, determine your level of prosperity in this life, and where you will spend eternity.

You might question, "But you said it was somebody he met at church." Please understand, not everyone joins a congregation for righteous reasons. Some people attend looking for a spouse, others for a job, still others to meet prospects so they can make a sale. In rare cases, people invade a church to find their next victim to scam. Pray and ask the Lord to give you discernment.

The Realm Of Partnership

The blessings of God move beyond labor and connection—they take us into the realm of a covenant partnership.

Yes, Abraham was linked to Melchizedek, the Lord's representative, but he also partnered together with God Most High.

You may ask, "Why does God need representatives?"

Above all else, the Almighty cares about His Word reaching as many as possible. God could bless you with incredible abundance, yet it is a small matter in the entity called "The Kingdom of God."

The Lord's primary concern is getting His message out to the masses, so people can come to a saving knowledge of His Son. If, in the process, He blesses you along the way, what a bonus!

The Master's Plan

God has a divine plan for finances to flow into His Kingdom—to purchase land, build churches and spread the Word through media. How? By blessing His people—just as He did with Abraham—so we will have a tithe to give.

Since the Father does not randomly drop gold coins from heaven, the only method He has for transferring wealth for His purpose is by causing His sons and daughters to experience abundance and financially support His work. So God is looking for Abraham-type people today—individuals who are not afraid of labor and are willing to become associated with modern-day Melchizedeks.

How The Lord Spoke To Me

When these principles are put into operation, miracles begin to happen.

In February of 1997, I was preaching in Mombasa, Kenya, when the Lord spoke to me concerning helping missionary Bud Sickler build the dream of his lifelong work—a large new church facility.

God dealt with me concerning the fact the construction could begin if there was enough money for the roof—the most expensive part of the project. Then the Lord said, "I want your congregation to provide the money for his dream to come to reality."

My immediate response was, "Yes, Lord. But we're talking about $500,000."

God responded to my spirit, "I know how much it is, just go ahead and do it. This will be the easiest thing you have ever done. And I will help you."

So, in February of 1997, I accepted God's "faith challenge."

How Big Is Your Promise To God?

It took only sixteen months for our congregation to give the needed amount—and we paid the entire $500,000 by June, 1998. Then, in December of 1999, I received a call from missionary Sickler who told me, "I thought we could get the steel into the country without paying duty, but Kenya is facing economic trouble and we have to pay duty. The roof is now going to total $600,000."

I was polite, but have to admit I got off the phone as quickly as possible.

God May Test You!

When I put the receiver down, I looked up to the heavens and said, "Lord, that's *his* problem. You told me to give a half-million dollars and that's exactly what I did!"

God responded, "What kind of a partner are you? One who goes only part of the way?"

Rather offended, I replied, "No, of course not."

Then the Lord continued, "For you to accomplish what I have called you to do, you will need partners to stand with you until the last bill is paid. But to *have* that, you must *be* that."

In January, 2000, I stood before our congregation and announced, "We need another $100,000 to finish the roof in Kenya." Through a divine miracle of giving, the entire amount was raised in two services one Sunday morning.

I called Bud Sickler with the good news and joyfully told him I would be bringing the funds the next week (on a mission trip which had already been scheduled).

Little did I know just a few days later, this dear, dedicated missionary would pass from this life into eternity. Thanks be to God, his dream was completed before he died

When we reached Mombasa, I handed the final check to his widow,

Fay. At that point I thought we were finished with the project. However, when Sue and I returned three months later for the official building dedication, we discovered there were other cost overruns—to the tune of $60,000. And, of course, in the natural I thought, "Here we go again!"

When we arrived home, our church graciously gave once more. This time, it was $10,000 to go with $50,000 which had already been pledged from other sources. I said, "Finally! It's done!"

It's Over When God Says It's Over

The Lord was not finished. The next time I journeyed to Mombasa I discovered there was one more additional bill we did not know about—a retainer on the steel in the amount of $17,000. The Lord said, "Pay it!"—and showed me how!

God instructed me to have a "Finish it, seed faith offering." He said, "Everybody in the congregation has something they have been believing for. Now is their time to receive it—and have that dream behind them."

The next Sunday, on the Lord's direction, I stood before our congregation and said, "I am asking for 170 people who will give exactly $100 as an act of faith so whatever you have been believing God for, you will receive—and the Lord will say 'It is finished.'"

My wife and I gave $100 in each of the three morning services, and so did many others. The amount to finish the Kenya project was completed.

Today, I have a letter from Joshua Akali, the African pastor of the Mombasa church thanking us for being used of God. Attached is a note from the architect certifying all the bills for the church are indeed, "Paid in full." Hallelujah!

Because we were faithful in obeying God in giving, the Lord began to financially bless our church in unexpected ways. The outpouring of His abundance has never stopped.

CHAPTER THREE

"BLESSED BY THE GREATER"

Believers will often read a passage in the Old Testament and say, "Since this is in the old covenant and not the new, it doesn't apply to my life."

This is simply an argument of convenience for a topic such individuals do not wish to come to terms with in their personal lives.

We have been reading what Genesis 14 has to say regarding walking in financial covenant with God. However, Hebrews 7 is a commentary on this exact subject.

A prelude to this topic is found in the last part of Hebrews 6, dealing with the High Priesthood of the Lord Jesus Christ. It is vital for every Christian to understand: *"When God made his promise to Abraham, since there was no one greater for him to swear by, he swore by himself, saying, 'I will surely bless you and give you many descendants.' And so after waiting patiently, Abraham received what was promised. Men swear by someone greater than themselves, and the oath confirms what is said and puts an end to all argument. Because God wanted to make the unchanging nature of his purpose very clear to the heirs of what was promised, he confirmed it with an oath. God did this so that, by two unchangeable things in which it is impossible for God to lie, we who have fled to take hold of the hope offered to us may be greatly encouraged. We have this hope as an anchor for the soul, firm and secure. It enters the inner sanctuary behind the curtain, where Jesus, who went before us, has entered on our behalf. He has become a high priest forever, in the order of Melchizedek"* (Hebrews 6:13-20).

Here, in the New Testament, referring to the eternal priesthood of the Lord Jesus Christ, reference is made of the man to whom Abraham paid his tithe, Melchizedek. Even more, the Lord has become a High Priest *"forever."*

Then, because the writer of Hebrews makes mention of Melchizedek, he feels compelled to explain what he is talking about. That's why we have recorded in Hebrews 7 the story of Melchizedek, priest of God Most High.

Jesus, The High Priest

The narration begins, *"This Melchizedek was king of Salem and priest of God Most High. He met Abraham returning from the defeat of the kings and blessed him, and Abraham gave him a tenth of everything. First, his name means 'king of righteousness'; then also, 'king of Salem' means 'king of peace.' Without father or mother, without genealogy, without beginning of days or end of life, like the Son of God he remains a priest forever"* (Hebrews 7:1-3).

Here we discover Melchizedek is a type—a foreshadowing—of

Christ. He is called "king of Salem" and "king of peace" and there is no record of his genealogy. When you read the book of Genesis, Melchizedek shows up out of the blue! This is exactly how the Lord Jesus appeared to the Jews in His day. If they had used our modern vernacular, they might have said, "Where did this guy come from?" Yet, Melchizedek is called a priest of God *forever.*

The writer of Hebrews goes on to speak of the greatness of Melchizedek. Think about it! As outstanding and noteworthy as Abraham was—a patriarch, the "father of our faith"—yet even so he had a relationship with another man the New Testament calls "great"! Scripture says: *"Just think how great he was: Even the patriarch Abraham gave him a tenth of the plunder! Now the law requires the descendants of Levi who become priests to collect a tenth from the people—that is, their brothers—even though their brothers are descended from Abraham. This man, however, did not trace his descent from Levi, yet he collected a tenth from Abraham and blessed him who had the promises"* (vv.4-6).

Many miss God because they believe, "Tithing is under the law—and since we are no longer under the law, I am not bound by such a covenant." However, by using this rationalization, they fail to receive God's financial best for their lives! Again, tithing *preceded* the Law. Now in the New Testament, the Word explains that Abraham gave a tithe to the priest Melchizedek before Levi was even born! This was also prior to Moses—who wrote and codified the law. And since the writer of Hebrews is now speaking of tithing in the New Testament, we know it *succeeded* the law.

Tithing Is God's Law Of Prosperity

It is clear that when we refer to tithing, we are not speaking of the moral law of Moses, or the Levitical law—those having to do with the diet and how we wash our hands. No, tithing refers to another kind of mandate. We need to realize there are many principles God set in motion at creation which have not passed out of effect—including the law of gravity and of sowing and reaping. So it is with His command of tithing—which is nothing more than the financial version of the law of sowing and reaping.

As Melchizedek blessed Abraham, the lesser must be blessed by the greater! Scripture records that after the priest collected the tithe, he *"...blessed him who had the promises. And without doubt the lesser person is blessed by the greater. In the one case, the tenth is collected by men who die; but in the other case, by him who is declared to be living"* (Hebrews 7:6-8).

The important point is: Jesus, our High Priest, is the one to whom we are presenting our tithe. Look at the verse again: *"In the one case* [the Old Testament], *the tenth is collected by men who die; but in the other case* [the New Testament], *by him who is declared to be living"* (v.8).

More Than a Contract

A financial covenant is vital. Why? Because if you see the blessing of God as being a hit-and-miss lottery, you will spend your entire life living in the realm of luck. Christianity, then, is no different to you than a spiritual version of Las Vegas. But *partnership* with God is much more.

A covenant is an agreement between a lesser and a greater party. This is different than a contract—an agreement between two equal parties. Hence, a contract can be negotiated, re-negotiated, or purposefully breached without harm. But a covenant "comes down" from authority, and the greater party dictates the terms, while the lesser either agrees or refuses to commit.

Any time man has dealings with God, it is in the realm of covenant, because Jehovah will negotiate with no man. You cannot discuss the terms of your salvation or any other aspect of your relationship with God. You either enter into His covenants, or you do not. It is just that simple.

This is why the Bible declares, *"But remember the Lord your God, for it is he who gives you the ability to produce wealth* [The King James says: "The power to produce wealth."]*...and so confirms his covenant, which he swore to your forefathers, as it is today"* (Deuteronomy 8:18).

We are not discussing living the Christian life as some kind of spiritual "freeloader." No, we're talking about tithing—a *covenant* of prosperity wherein God gives you the power and ability to produce wealth.

Make this confession: "I'm not a moocher. I am a producer."

The Lord expects us to generate more than we use. Why is this the will of God for our lives? So we will not only have the money to tithe, but also enough to give offerings into God's Gospel. Plus, the Lord wants you to provide for your family and lend rather than borrow. As the Bible says, *"The Lord will open the heavens, the storehouse of his bounty, to send rain on your land in season and to bless all the work of your hands. You will lend to many nations but will borrow from none"* (Deuteronomy 28:12).

Your Creator desires that you have *more* than you need so you can always be generous—with your family and with God. The apostle Paul writes, *"You will be made rich in every way so that you can be generous on every occasion, and through us your generosity will result in thanksgiving to God"* (2 Corinthians 9:11).

Your Source

I believe it is time for God's people to get out of their "moocher" mentality and understand that they have been called by Almighty God to walk in a financial covenant with Him. The Lord is your source, not man. This partnership brings an assurance that God will bless whatever you put your hands to—and elevate you into a realm where you are always progressing forward financially and spiritually.

There are only three things which can sabotage your walking independently in financial covenant with God Most High:

1. Not knowing about such a covenant from the Word of God.
2. Not doing your part in upholding this covenant (because if you fail to do your part, God will not do His).
3. Acting devoid of faith, or "just going through the motions."

Some people go to work "religiously," come to church "religiously" and even tithe "religiously." How do we know when a person appears to be *doing* the right thing, but in an attitude without faith? The evidence is their lack of enthusiasm. If you *believe* God is blessing you *as* you work, attend church or tithe, you will obviously be excited.

I tell those in our congregation, "Don't tithe religiously, tithe *faithfully*. Because, if it is something you do monotonously or grudgingly, there will be zero power attached to your actions.

Whatever you do for God you must do in faith believing."

In our church we declare a faith confession each time we receive tithes and offerings. Why? Because we're not just glibly giving—we are joyfully giving in faith. We believe that when we wake up on Monday morning and go to work, we will be more productive with God's hand resting upon us than we ever could be without His touch!

It is the Lord who gives us the ability to produce—the power to attain wealth.

Greater Than Your Own

There are those who cannot walk in the covenantal blessings of God because they are unwilling to admit there is any business on the earth greater than their own.

It does not matter if you are a heart surgeon or the CEO of a Fortune 500 corporation. Your business is not as great as God's business. What our Heavenly Father is interested in is that no one would perish, but all would come to a saving knowledge of His Son. Perhaps, a surgeon can repair a fleshly heart, but what benefit is it if the patient goes to hell five years later?

God doesn't mind blessing you with material abundance, if it will get your attention and empower you to give into the Gospel. However, what the Lord *does* mind is you being selfish and consuming for yourself one hundred percent of everything you earn.

Your Business Is Your Business—To A Point

Several years ago there was a man in our ministry who entered into immorality. When I called his hand, he retorted, "Well, that's none of your business!"

I replied, "You are exactly right. Your business *is* your business—but right up to the point where your business trespasses on mine. Because my business is higher than your business."

I told him, "If you want to sleep with another man's wife, find someone out in the world to satisfy your urges. Don't enter the House of God and pick on one of these handmaidens of the Lord. When you do, you are on *my* turf. And when this happens you are automatically playing by my rules."

The truth that the Lord is above all should encourage and empower you. How can you be blessed "by the greater" if you never admit there *is* anyone greater? This is why some people *cannot* walk in the blessings of God.

Do What the Lord Wants

Far too many of God's people are "believing Him for a miracle" while at the same time they are doing absolutely nothing for the Kingdom. They are not prayer counselors, helpers in Children's Church, greeters or ushers in the house of the Lord—and are not tithing. In addition there are those who are not holding down steady jobs—just waiting for some unexpected monetary surprise.

Zig Ziglar says, "A lot of people are waiting for their ship to come in. But the trouble is, they never sent one out!"

What many Christians fail to grasp is, a large financial reaping comes only from big sowing—not wasting time waiting for a "harvest" which will never arrive.

Let me emphasize again God funds His Gospel by *blessing* the work of His people. And tithing brings supernatural blessing on the labor!

Yes, the Lord understands you have to make a mortgage payment, pay taxes and buy shoes for your children. So, how can God help you do all of that, *plus* have enough to give Him a tenth of everything which crosses your hands, and have even more left over to give offerings of love and thanksgiving in His Gospel and to invest in savings? The answer is, the Lord blesses the labor of those who dare to walk independently in financial covenant with Him.

People have such funny ideas about *how* God is going to bless them. During the Y2K scare of the Millennium, there was actually a television evangelist preaching, "The finance companies are going to have computer troubles and lose track of all the mortgages records. This is how the Father is going to bless His people."

What misguided thinking! It was one more excuse to avoid the Lord's *real* plan for getting wealth into the hands of His people.

God Will Give You Creative Ideas

As you walk independently in financial covenant with God Most High, He will give you more creative ideas and insight which will allow you to work at a higher, more efficient level. You will inevitably produce and earn more than you ever thought possible. Why? Because you can have greater accomplishments with the hand of God upon you than you could ever achieve without Him.

I learned years ago if someone gets upset over the blessings of God in my life they're not a tither, because a giver would understand the favor of God. Tithers would say to themselves, "The pastor has been sowing, therefore, he is reaping."

They understand the principle, while others don't. It has always been this way; if you let critical people know you are tithing, they think you're crazy. And when the blessings of God arrive, you will be shocked to hear what terrible things they are saying about you!

The world only comprehends action on the human level—manipulating the system, placating the boss against their better judgment or getting another person to do something for them. However, what we are discussing is directing our positive attention toward the Lord—being a *doer* of the Word and daring to believe God will *bless* us for it!

What a marvelous way to live!

Chapter Four

God's Method of Provision for His People

Just after my wife and I were married, we had a difficult time borrowing $350 for a sofa. A banker finally made us deposit $350 in an account before he would loan us the same amount for the piece of furniture. That's what it took to establish our credit.

After we paid the debt, the same banker approved us for a Visa card, but placed a $250 limit on the account.

How things have changed! From the moment our son became a student at Texas Christian University, he began to receive offers from MasterCard, Visa and Discover practically every week—all wanting to give him sure and easy credit. It's no wonder the average college student graduates with over $10,000 in credit card debt, not counting school loans.

This shows how the world's monetary system wraps its tentacles around the latest generation more decisively than ever before. My grandfather, who survived the Great Depression as a farmer, would have never thought of borrowing money for a new truck. No, if he purchased a vehicle, it had to be with cash. Land was the only exception on which he would even consider carrying debt.

Under the world's system of money, if they can entice you into debt, they can—and will—control you. I'm sure you know someone who has worked thirty, forty or fifty years on a job and still has no financial freedom. Their "golden years" are anything but, because they are destined to an existence of scraping by.

Consider the stock bubble of the late 1990s which peaked in March of 2000. By July 2002, fully one-half of all the gains made by the *Standard & Poor 500* during the entire bull market of 1982 to 2000 were wiped out. That's the world's system! You think you have accumulated wealth, then "Poof!" it's gone!

A Tenth Of The Plunder

Why is it so difficult for people to escape this trap? The reason is they are only living in the realm of labor and they have never entered into the realm of "plunder." Notice what scripture says: *"...Abraham gave him a tenth of the plunder!"* (Hebrews 7:4). It's a truth we will deal with later in this chapter.

You may ask, "What about Christians? Shouldn't they be better equipped to gain financial independence through their relationship with God by faith in Jesus Christ?"

We all know individuals who attend church every week, labor their whole lives, but are never able to break out of "the system."

Why does this happen even to God's people? It's because they live at the level of their own intellect rather than at the place of the

Father's plan for them.

Your Unlimited Future

One man labors and stays in the system; another man labors, yet he breaks free. What is the difference? The one who is liberated goes to work on Monday fully aware, absolutely convinced, that he does not work as other men do, rather he works in partnership with the Most High God. The next man toils on his own—at the level or limit of his personal intellect and ability.

The reason you are unlimited is because you are not going to your place of employment on your own, but in covenant partnership with the Lord your God, and therefore are not held back by your ability or education. You operate at a supernatural level because it is the Almighty who gives you the power to produce wealth *"and so confirms his covenant"* (Deuteronomy 8:18).

God's Partnership Base

Let's say God one day decides, "I need to get an extra million dollars to the ministry of Pastor Lingerfelt at Overcoming Faith Christian Center in Arlington, Texas."

Well, how is the Lord going to accomplish this? He looks in the midst of the congregation—the partnership base—to find people who qualify. They must be believers who are working, tithing and walking by faith in the Word of God. Then, He says, "I will somehow bless their lives so they are able to produce and generate an extra ten million dollars."

Why ten million, when the church only needs *one* million? God does not mind His people keeping the ninety percent so long as they are willing and obedient to give the ten percent. If Christians understood this they would be rejoicing rather than complaining about "paying the tithe."

God does not work through credit and control; rather, God works through blessing and liberty.

Supernatural Increase

You may not reap a harvest every day, but you *can* labor each day—in partnership with God. Then, as you work, by faith your efforts will be blessed by the Father. This is now your needs are met week after week.

Subsequently, as you present your tithe, there will be those occasions when you will come into the thirty-fold, sixty-fold and even one hundred-fold harvest which propels you out of the world's system of money, credit and control.

One of the major reasons I am writing this book is because I don't want you to use your divine harvest to pay past debts. I want to show you how to eliminate them so your increase can be used as God intends. He desires to propel you to the next financial level.

"Above And Beyond"

In the book of Matthew we read the story of Peter, who needed to pay some taxes, so he went to the Lord with his dilemma. Jesus said to him, *"But so that we may not offend them, go to the lake and throw out your line. Take the first fish you catch; open its mouth and you will find a four-drachma coin. Take it and give it to them for my tax and yours."* (Matthew 17:27).

What are the odds of finding such a valuable coin in a fish's mouth—especially the *first* fish you caught?

If Peter had been walking by his own intellect, he would have left the tax bill unpaid. The same would be true if he had gone fishing (laboring) in his own ability and strength.

The Lord, however, does not call on us to walk by human reasoning, rather by faith. This is why some never break out of the mold. They refuse to believe there is an Intellect at work in the universe greater than their own. Personally, I don't need to understand everything in order to succeed.

My son once asked me, "Dad, how can you run the television department when you don't know what's going on in there?"

I answered, "I don't *want* to know how videos are duplicated. If I did, I might want to get involved—which would take me away from God's calling on my ministry."

As long as I study and pray, our ministry operates "out of the box."

Think about the daily activities you engage in without understanding how they really work. Do you comprehend how tumblers operate in a lock when you try to open your front door? Yet you use the key. Do you really know what happens when you turn the ignition switch to drive your vehicle? Yet you drive your car. Or, do you really understand how a brown cow can eat green grass and produce white milk? Yet you drink the milk!

I don't need to understand how God blesses my life. Rather, I am to be as a child, willing and obedient to my Father.

Walking By Faith

Natural thinking and actions yield natural results. But faith thinking and actions yield the results of faith—the promises of the

Word of God.

The steps taken by Abraham are the basic principles by which the Lord blesses His people today.

Genesis 26 describes a great drought which left the people without food. The Bible records, *"Now there was a famine in the land—besides the earlier famine of Abraham's time—and Isaac went to Abimelech king of the Philistines in Gerar. The Lord appeared to Isaac and said, 'Do not go down to Egypt; live in the land where I tell you to live. Stay in this land for a while, and I will be with you and will bless you. For to you and your descendants I will give all these lands and will confirm the oath I swore to your father Abraham. I will make your descendants as numerous as the stars in the sky and will give them all these lands, and through your offspring all nations on earth will be blessed, because...'"* (Genesis 26:1-5).

We Are Blessed—"Because"

When I come across a word like "because" in the Word of God, I am curious. I don't just read the Bible, I study it. If I find a *result* in scripture, I desire to know how it came about. For example, if there is a healing, I want to discover *how* the person in the Bible received his miracle. If there's a financial blessing, I want to know *how* it happened.

I continued reading and learned that through Abraham's offspring, *"all nations on earth will be blessed because Abraham obeyed me and kept my requirements, my commands, my decrees and my laws"* (v.5).

God is saying to Isaac, "Don't go down to Egypt—where your mind says to go, or because everyone else is headed there in search of food." Instead, the Lord promised, "If you will stay in the land I will bless you."

Isaac not only had the faith to listen to God, but the Bible records, *"Isaac planted crops in that land..."* (v.12). What land? The land of famine and hunger. Next we learn: *"the same year* [he] *reaped a hundredfold because the Lord blessed him"* (v.12).

What year? The same year as the great drought.

Isaac did not have a hundredfold harvest because he was a skilled farmer—or because of his knowledge of agriculture or pure luck. It was because *"the Lord blessed him."*

This is God's method of moving abundance to His people and into His Kingdom. You are not going to walk out in the morning and find gold Krugerrands strewn on the lawn like dew. But God will put His hand of anointing and favor on your life so when you labor you will be productive and blessed.

More Than Enough

When you understand and follow God's financial plan—that He blesses your *labor*—you will be propelled up into the next level, the occasions when you reap a supernatural financial harvest from God's hand.

Next, we learn this about Isaac: *"The man became rich..."* (v,13). Obviously, this was not an inheritance. If so, why would the Bible record his financial circumstances this way? Isaac must have turned around and sold those crops to the Philistines and gathered up all of their money.

His riches were above and beyond what Abraham left him, because we read, *"The man became rich, and his wealth continued to grow until he became very wealthy"* (v.13).

Since God uses the terms "rich," "wealth" and "wealthy" so often in the Word, a person would have to be intellectually dishonest to come to the conclusion the Lord doesn't want His people to prosper—to have *more than enough.*

Your Objective is Prosperity

Isaac *"had so many flocks and herds and servants that the Philistines envied him"* (v.14).

Your command to prosper is not complete until the "Philistines" in your city become jealous of you. The Lord desires for people of every nation to know there is only one Living God—the only true God who answers prayer.

Unbelievers are not interested in your faith as long as you are having to jumpstart your car every time you get in it—or you are living beneath their lifestyle. They are thinking, "Before you tell me about your God, get your act together!"

You Are Not Limited

The Lord desires for you to have an Isaac type of testimony. He wants the Amorites, Hittites, and Jebusites to sit up and take notice and see there's something different about you. Perhaps you have less education than they do, but still you're pulling ahead—always receiving promotions and raises. They will want to know, "What's going on?" And this will open the door for you to share that your blessings come from a partnership with God Almighty.

As we give the Lord a tenth of both our labor and our unexpected reaping, we will become the wealthiest Christian generation because we will give up our "poverty mentality" once and for all and embrace God's principles of the harvest.

The Lord *will* bless His people as we cooperate with His financial plan for our lives.

The real questions are: If God were looking to get an extra million dollars into His ministry, would He even consider using you? Could He know with absolute certainty that if He put ten million extra dollars into your hands, you would give His Gospel a tithe? Or would you consume your "seed corn"? Would you spend all you receive on your own human wants and desires?

If you cannot be counted faithful by God, you will live the rest of your days without experiencing a single financial miracle. Why? Because God cannot trust you!

Many Christians "kid themselves" saying when they become financially secure, *then* they will tithe and be a blessing to the church. However, if the Lord can't trust you with ten dollars, why would He entrust you with a hundred? If God can't have confidence in your tithing on a thousand dollars, why would He trust you with a million?

Your Provider and Protector

What was true of Isaac was true of his father, Abraham: *"The Lord had said to Abraham, 'Leave your country, your people and your father's household and go to the land I will show you...'"* Why leave? Because you need to learn you're not dependent on others, not even Mom or Dad. You must discover how to relate to God as your *Source*!

The Lord not only told Abraham He would make him a great nation, but also said, *"I will bless those who bless you, and whoever curses you I will curse..."* (Genesis 12:3). Applying these words to your own life, you don't need to worry about office politics or someone trying to target you. Because when you walk in financial covenant with the Lord, God is not only your *Provider*, He is also your *Protector*.

When people dare to point their finger of condemnation at you, they are harming their own future since they will be judged by God. This is one more benefit of walking in financial covenant with the Father.

Abraham's Plunder

Now the Bible says Abraham gave Melchizedek a tenth of the plunder. What is "plunder"? It is those occasions when you walk into that thirty, sixty, and one hundred-fold harvest.

I realize there are people who believe there is no such thing, but as I wrote in my book, *Four Steps to Prosperity Now*, "Oops, too late!" I've already experienced a sixty-fold return!

In 1993 I gave the Lord $15,000 in a "challenge offering" and God miraculously gave me more than a sixty-fold return inside of sixty days. If someone was going to tell me not to believe in such a thing, they should have told me earlier. It's too late now!

Many Christians *talk faith*, but they *walk in poverty*. The reason is that they do not see how God blesses their labor.

Act on the Word

Abraham was a shepherd, and God blessed him in his endeavors. He also had to dig water wells in order to survive in the desert—and again the Lord blessed him. *Whatever* Abraham put his hands to prospered.

His recovered plunder after the battle at Sodom was an extra, supernatural harvest, above and beyond his day-to-day work. As the apostle Paul writes, *"If a man will not work, he shall not eat"* (2 Thessalonians 3:10).

Even if God gave the average Christian a multiple harvest it would do little good since most are so far underwater financially, they are drowning in a sea of debt! However, if a person will dare to *act* on the Word and *partner* their lives together with God financially, they can be blessed in all their labor and thereby keep current with their financial needs.

The plan of God is that you be blessed day-by-day, week-by-week—and for eternity.

Chapter Five

Making Your Life Productive

What amazing potential we have when we decide to partner our lives with the Living God!

Somehow, this concept has been lost to our generation, yet the reality is that the Bible records many accounts of God intervening favorably in the affairs of men and women who build their lives on His precepts. Abraham and Isaac are two such people.

The "father of nations" witnessed how God supernaturally assists His people by transferring abundance from sinners to saints. As King Solomon would later write, *"A good man leaves an inheritance for his children's children, but a sinner's wealth is stored up for the righteous"* (Proverbs 13:22).

Renewing Your Covenant With God

Genesis 15 begins with two telling words: *"After this..."* After what? It speaks of the events following the time Abraham renewed his financial covenant by giving a tithe. He then received a fresh word from the Lord.

Here is what took place. *"After this, the word of the Lord came to Abraham in a vision: Do not be afraid, Abraham. I am your shield, your very great reward"* (Genesis 15:1).

In this one verse God communicates three principles to His chosen servant. First, God says to Abraham, *"Do not be afraid."*

The reason I have emphasized the word *"independently"* throughout this book is because when you walk in covenant with God you are not financially dependent on others and you fear no man.

"Independent" does not mean "arrogant." Instead of being ungrateful, we thank our Heavenly Father for our employment. And if we work for an honest company and have reputable superiors, we appreciate that too—yet they are not our ultimate source.

The world can do what it wants, but the people of God who practice these principles are going to prosper. Negative things may be swirling all around, yet it does not adversely affect them because they are *independently* walking in financial covenant with God Most High.

This is why Jehovah reassuringly tells him, "Abraham, do not be afraid." When you make your pact with God, you lose your fear. We know *"that in all things God works for the good of those who love him, who have been called according to his purpose"* (Romans 8:28).

In the midst of devastating circumstances you can be assured of two things: (1) God did not cause the problem and (2) the Almighty will show up in your time of need and turn it around for good.

Your Shield and Reward

The second principle God communicates to Abraham is *"I am your shield"* (Genesis 15:1). He is saying, "No harm can come your way because I am your protcction."

Finally, the third principle the Lord shared was, He is *"...your very great reward"* (v.1).

I don't know about you, but I would much rather receive a reward from the hand of God than General Motors, Xerox or the Ford Motor Company.

Abraham's recompense for entering into a financial covenant with God was far more beneficial than the perks any earthly corporation could possibly offer. He not only lost his fear, he had a shield of protection and the promise of a great reward.

Remember the Lord Your God—Always!

We are not to sit idly by, waiting for wealth to drop into our lap or be consumed in a search for riches. And we certainly are not to jeopardize our integrity by "sucking up" to others in an attempt to curry their favor in order to secure material abundance. No, as people who walk in covenant with the Lord, we *produce* wealth.

Consider a fallow field—ground which has not been cultivated and does not have a crop growing on it. Suppose some hard working individual went to that land, and by the sweat of his brow, plows and sows seed for the purpose of producing a harvest. Would the earth care whether the person was white, black, male, female, tall, short, fat, thin, rich or poor? Absolutely not! The soil is not prejudiced, it simply awaits someone—*anyone*—to come along and make it productive.

So it is in your life!

However, you may ask: "Besides tilling, what does the farmer have to do to make the earth produce?"

There is only one requirement—he must sow a seed.

Are You Productive?

Your life represents the soil—and the Word of God is the fertile seed.

Jesus spoke of this in the Parable of the Sower. It concerned a farmer who scattered his seed. Some fell on a path and the birds came and ate it; some fell on rocky places where there wasn't much soil—and the plants withered and died. Other seed fell among thorns, which grew up and choked the plants.

However, the seed which fell on good soil *"...came up, grew and produced a crop, multiplying thirty, sixty, or even a hundred times"* (Mark 4:8).

Jesus gave an explanation of the parable, saying, *"The farmer sows the word"* (v.14). Then, He states, *"Some people* [we will call this Group One] *are like seed along the path, where the word is sown. As soon as they hear it, Satan comes and takes away the word that was sown in them"* (v.15).

What does the devil desperately want to remove? God's Word!

Jesus continues, *"Others,* [we will call this Group Two] *like seed sown on rocky places, hear the word and at once receive it with joy. But since they have no root, they last only a short time. When trouble or persecution comes because of the word, they quickly fall away"* (vv.16-17).

Yes, the Word stirs up the enemy and causes persecution and there are those who will flee.

However, *"Still others,* [Group Three] *like seed sown among thorns, hear the word; but the worries of this life, the deceitfulness of wealth and the desires for other things come in and choke the word, making it unfruitful"* (vv.18-19).

The objective of Satan is found in the last three words of this verse: "*...making it* [the soil or a person's life] *unfruitful."* It is the devil's desire—and contrary to the Will of God—to cause such a negative result.

Next we read, *"Others,* [Group Four] *like seed sown on good soil, hear the word, accept it, and produce a crop—thirty, sixty or even a hundred times what was sown"* (v.20).

What a harvest!

God's Expectation for You

I am not asking you to wait for some miracle increase. Rather I am encouraging you to *produce* a thirty, sixty or one-hundred fold return. There is a profound difference!

I don't expect wealth to knock on my door or be delivered by FedEx. I go out to work—and as a result, I have the hand of the Lord and the anointing of the Spirit on my life. This is how I can enter a "dry place" and produce an abundant yield. God says I will *"...be like a shelter from the wind and a refuge from the storm, like streams of water in the desert and the shadow of a great rock in a thirsty land"* (Isaiah 32:2).

This is what a farmer does when he goes into *"a parched and barren land"* (Joel 2:20). The dry ground has no crop, yet the farmer forces the earth into production.

You Must Listen

The key to your harvest is to hear and retain the Word. Remember the teaching of Jesus: *"Others, like seed sown on good soil, hear the word, accept it, and produce a crop..."* (Mark 4:20).

This is exactly what Isaac did. He listened and obeyed what the Lord had to say. How do we know Isaac accepted God's counsel? Because he stayed in Gerar rather than flee to Egypt (Genesis 26:6). It was his first step to receiving a bountiful blessing.

Many want a "miracle return," yet don't want to *hear* God.

In the past, I have made the same mistake—hearing from the Lord but ignoring His counsel. And it was during those moments I experienced shortage instead of surplus.

The world says, "timing is everything," but I choose to believe hearing God's voice is everything. Why? Because when you listen for and accept His direction, you will *automatically* be in the right place at the right time.

There has been much criticism concerning the thirty, sixty and one hundred-fold return, but it is biblical teaching—and I have the right to believe God for such abundance.

Don't Destroy the Potential

Every precious life leaving a hospital nursery has great potential. It does not really matter one's ethnic or economic background. However, in order to ruin their lives someone has to negatively influence them—with drugs, custody battles, abuse, criticism or misguided teaching.

In order to make children unproductive, you've got to go out of your way to damage them morally, emotionally, educationally or physically.

To be productive is the *norm*—and is the Will of God. The Almighty has literally "programmed" His entire creation to be producers. Yet, *"...the devil prowls around like a roaring lion looking for someone to devour"* (1 Peter 5:8).

Of course, Satan often focuses his attention on children because if he can wound them, they will never be a threat to him and his agenda as they enter into adulthood. This is why every righteous ministry prays to be a blessing to children—before gangs, drugs or other sin gets a grip on their lives. They are our future.

What are you doing to help make the soil around you productive?

Chapter Six

The Most Important Prosperity Message You Have Ever Heard

My blessings are not dependent upon man, but on my partnership with God—believing His Word is exalted above all my circumstances.

I am learning to follow the example of King David when he wrote, *"I will bow down toward your holy temple and will praise your name for your love and your faithfulness, for you have exalted above all things your name and your word"* (Psalm 138:2).

Negative events may happen—from terror bombings to hurricanes—yet as I walk in covenant with God, *"A thousand may fall at* [my] *side, ten thousand at* [my] *right hand, but...no harm will befall* [me], *no disaster will come near* [my] *tent"* (Psalm 91:7,10).

Watch Your Environment

In our ministry, every week of every year we encourage people to strive for God's best. Those who attend our church know we will be preaching a message of faith, hope, abundance, prosperity, fidelity, health and virtue. We are not there to entertain people or win a popularity contest.

As people begin to build their lives around such a message, they start performing at the level they are hearing Sunday after Sunday—and it begins to be demonstrated in their lifestyles.

Churches are much like restaurants. They have a certain standard of food, service and clientele. And when your spiritual taste buds get used to a five-star faith environment, you are no longer satisfied returning to a place serving nothing but "sugar food" and intellectual pablum.

If you are a new Christian it is difficult to find the right church to attend. Personally, I *must* have a faith-based diet each and every week. Every believer should worship in a place where a scripture-based overcoming lifestyle is the focus.

In ministry we meet people who have spiritual problems, but they fail to seek God or read His Holy Word. They have serious financial difficulties, yet somehow they refuse to work.

There are some things you don't need a Ph.D. to figure out! If you are unemployed, you're going to have unmet needs. And, if you fail to pray, of course, you will feel disconnected from God.

Where Will You Go From Here?

If you leave a faith-filled environment and switch to a "Let's-Preach-What's-Popular," or a "Sympathy International" ministry, you are going to suffer spiritually. It's like trading steak for doughnuts!

The anointing of God comes by association and environment. So if you desire to learn how to walk in covenant with God, it is vital to pay attention to these factors.

People are defeated because they align themselves with negative ministries and pessimistic "friends."

Becoming "Blessed" By God

Covenental power is based on the Word of God. David begins the book of Psalms with these words: *"Blessed is the man* [or, "the person"] *that walketh not in the counsel of the ungodly, nor standeth in the way of sinners, nor sitteth in the seat of the scornful. But his delight is in the law of the Lord; and in his law doth he meditate day and night. And he shall be like a tree planted by the rivers of water, that bringeth forth his fruit in his season; his leaf also shall not wither; and whatsoever he doeth shall prosper"* (Psalm 1:1-3 KJV).

This should be our personal objective—to have a faith which produces. What you are learning will *protect* you in times of recession and *promote* you in times of expansion.

Full Speed Ahead!

I don't believe in downsizing, expecting less materially or spiritually. God is not in favor of having His children regress—*"...his leaf also shall not wither"* (v.3). Even in times of drought, the tree of prosperity and blessing stays green because it is planted by the river. In good times and bad, you will thrive.

How will this happen? Because you *do* something about your situation. The key word is *doeth—"whatsoever he doeth shall prosper"* (v.3).

Who Is Blessed?

The favor of the Father comes from delighting yourself in the law of God, not from:

- Walking in the counsel of the ungodly.
- Seeking out the fellowship of sinners.
- Sitting in the seat of the scornful—or "mockers."

You cannot simultaneously do these things and enjoy the covenant blessings of God.

I've met those who attend church every Sunday, and even tithe, yet they waste their spiritual efforts by complaining.

When the people of God constantly murmured against Moses and Aaron, they were not blessed; neither did they enter God's Promised Land. Instead, they died in the desert, never knowing the Lord's peace and rest.

They sabotaged their own lives and they negated the promises of God by their scornful behavior.

Here's what the Bible tells us: *"How oft did they provoke him in the wilderness, and grieve him in the desert! Yea, they turned back and tempted God, and limited the Holy One of Israel"* (Psalm 78:40-41 KJV).

What a difference in the behavior of a "blessed" person who has abundance and prosperity. They delight in God's Word and *"meditate night and day"* upon it (Psalm 1:2).

God's Success Formula

What we plant in our hearts through *meditation* eventually flows out of our mouths as *confession*. When God gave Joshua a success formula after the death of Moses, He said, *"Do not let this Book of the Law depart from your mouth; meditate on it day and night, so that you may be careful to do everything written in it. Then you will be prosperous and successful"* (Joshua 1:8).

Because the Lord desires for His children to prosper, He saw to it that His instructions to Joshua were recorded in scripture so you might read, believe and implement them. This is how you also can experience the same degree of blessing as God's servant, Joshua.

Be Connected!

Why is confession so important? Because the level of your faith will never rise above the level of your profession of the Word of God. The same is true of our fellowship "connections" or "associations."

If you wanted to learn how to play tennis, you wouldn't select the worst tennis player in the city to coach you. If you need a professional to assist you in selling your home you would be foolish to phone the local real estate board and ask, "Who sold the fewest homes in the city last year? That's who I want to hire to list my property!"

It's also true regarding your success. If you want to prosper in this life, find a Christian mentor—and someone who is doing better than yourself. Go to "school" under that person and apply what you learn.

Far too often people come into a faith-filled environment, yet waste their efforts because they simultaneously retain their sinful friends. They are running with the wrong crowd! Some even assume a 90-minute church service can more than overcome their entire week of a contradictory lifestyle.

If you're really committed to being a success with God, it's time to move away from your old negative connections.

Who's Your Advisor?

Psalm 1 is the most important prosperity message you will ever hear or read because it encompasses faith, giving and a host of success principles—resulting in becoming a blessed man or woman of God.

Most people understand they must do certain things to improve their lives for the better. However, few comprehend there are behaviors they must avoid.

Growing up, you were given all kinds of advice—by your parents, your teachers and in church. We then make the choice to decide which principles we will keep, and those we will discard. However, we cannot escape the direct command in scripture that we walk not in the counsel of the ungodly (Psalm 1.1).

Recently, a young married woman received advice at her workplace which led to the ruination of her marriage. Her boss told her she should open her own checking account, separate from her new husband. While there's nothing specifically wrong with such advice, it was none of her boss' business and was out of order for him to even raise the subject. The same executive told the woman she should insist on purchasing a different automobile and that it be titled in her name.

Unfortunately, this new bride was easily led. She did not think to ask herself, "What kind of agenda does my boss have? What are his intentions?"

She listened to the counsel of the ungodly and the results were disastrous.

Similar problems arise when we "stand in the way of sinners" (v.1)—or "hang out" with those who don't know the Lord.

Steer Clear of the Scornful

What else must we *not* do in order to have abundance in this life and be the success God desires us to be? We cannot "sit in the seat of the scornful" (v.1).

A "scornful" person is one you cannot make happy. Whatever you mention, they're against. You could turn on your television to a Christian station any time of the day and they are critical of whoever is conducting the program. They are perpetual faultfinders who rarely meet any individual they respect.

Such a person will cause a shipwreck of faith! Be wary of their influence.

The Best Odds for Success

God says He will meet all our needs, *"according to his glorious riches in Christ Jesus"* (Philippines 4:19). But how is the Lord going to accomplish this? The same God who gave us this promise also left instructions to provide for our own families as fulfillment of our faith and duty: *"But if any provide not for his own, and specially for those of his own house, he hath denied the faith, and is worse than an infidel"* (1 Thessalonians 5:8 KJV).

If we are diligent in our labor, "doers" of the Word and walk in financial covenant with Almighty God, He will work with us toward meeting all of our needs.

I once read a news article concerning a problem certain states are experiencing with lotteries. Apparently, when the jackpot grows extremely large, it causes major problems at convenience stores where the lines are sometimes three blocks long with people anxious to try their luck.

Personally, I wouldn't walk across the street to buy such a ticket—and the odds are thirty-million-to-one! That's not even gambling! If people understood the blessings of God, you wouldn't be able to find a seat in faith-filled churches and, believe you me, the lines would be *more* than three blocks long!

Why? Because we're not talking about odds of success which are thirty-million-to-one, or even three-to-one. The Word of God will work *every* time for those who are willing to "work" the Word!

It Takes Time

The laws of "seedtime and harvest" mean that what you plant in the spring you reap in the fall. Prospering by the labor of your hands may take time, but it is well worth the wait. As I tell my congregation, "Although you're probably not going to get rich by Tuesday putting into practice what I am preaching on Sunday—the Word always works!"

At the end of the year you will look back and say, "Lord, I can hardly believe how far you have brought me!" Plus, by being faithful, the blessings multiply year after year until you reach the point you no longer need to physically labor.

Get Near the River

My wife and I lived in Kenya when we served as missionaries, and I was a guest lecturer at a Bible college there.

During the dry season when we traveled out to the bush to look at the animals, the trees would be "browning out" as the drought set in. Most of the vegetation gave evidence it was in need of rain—except what was growing alongside the rivers. There, the trees were lush and green because the roots had spread out toward the flowing water.

Such trees are *independent* of the seasons. And that is what you can expect in your life if you follow the instruction of God's Word. You will be *"like a tree planted by rivers of water..."* (Psalm 1:3 KJV).

It's Your Season

You will also be a person who *"bringeth forth fruit in his season"* (v.3). Notice, you will not be producing the crop of others, based on *their* season—the timetable is *yours!* It was established by your covenant with God that you will give Him a tenth of everything that crosses your hands. And each time you give to the Lord, you are renewing this partnership. As a result, it produces a harvest.

Here's the exciting part: you do not lose what you accumulate through God's covenant. Remember, scripture declares, *"...his leaf also shall not wither"* (v.3). This means you move "upward and onward" every year, making constant progress and continually reaping. David also says of this blessed man, *"...and whatsoever he doeth shall prosper"* (v.3).

I've met those who say they want to get ahead, but their *actions* indicate otherwise. In order for your life to have productive power, your faith, your confession and your actions all need to be lined up and moving in the same direction.

Look in the Mirror

The principles we've been discussing are repeated in the New Testament by the writings of James. He counsels, *"Do not merely listen to the word, and so deceive yourselves. Do what it says. Anyone who listens to the word but does not do what it says is like a man who looks at his face in a mirror and, after looking at himself, goes away and immediately forgets what he looks like. But the man who looks intently into the perfect law that gives freedom* [the King James says "perfect law of liberty"] *and continues to do this not forgetting what he has heard, but doing it—he will be blessed in what he does"* (James 1:22-25).

This is what the Lord will do for anyone who dares to believe and act on His promises.

My wife and I were married at the age of twenty and moved a thousand miles from home. As we began a brand new life together, we made a covenant with the Lord and gave the Word of God first place in our lives. As we look back, the blessings are far too numerous to count.

What will you allow the Father to do for you?

Part Two

The God Touch

CHAPTER SEVEN

THE MIRACLE OF TITHING

In the remaining chapters I would like to share fifteen steps to help you reach that marvelous place in your life where others will conclude that you have been "touched by" or "blessed by" God.

The first of these is tithing.

No "Midas Touch"

I constantly mention the hand of God on His children—and on their labor—because it is *The God Touch.*

In times past I have heard Christian ministers refer to faith and prosperity teachings in a derogatory manner as "the Midas touch." Midas was a mythological Greek god-king who supposedly had the capacity to change everything he touched into gold. I have no idea why anyone would make such a comparison—for if your life *could* be touched by such a "god," you would eventually find yourself eternally separated from the true and living God.

How much better for your efforts and labor to be touched by the Creator. You will not only be blessed, but you'll be protected from difficulties: *"The blessing of the Lord brings wealth, and he adds no trouble to it"* (Proverbs 10:22).

Beyond Mere Working

Over the years, there have been those who complain, "Dr. Lingerfelt just wants people to be healthy, wealthy and wise. He goes around encouraging people and getting everyone's hopes up."

If that's an indictment, I'm guilty. I am standing on God's Word which declares, *"Beloved, I wish above all things that thou mayest prosper and be in health, even as thy soul prospereth"* (3 John 2 KJV).

Looking back on my journey, I have literally been on my own since the age of eighteen. Even before I was a teenager, I sold Christmas cards in our Detroit, Michigan neighborhood in the fall of each year. Then, when I was old enough, I started delivering newspapers for the *Detroit Free Press*—which had to be on doorsteps by 5:30 A.M. On many snowy winter mornings I had to put the papers on a sled and pull them over ice-covered roads to make the rounds.

I have *always* worked, yet I look around and see people who have labored their entire lives and have never advanced or accumulated anything substantial. Some have grey hair and are still paying rent for an apartment.

You see, it *is* possible to work and never progress. So there is obviously a difference between working and being *blessed* in your labor. Why go through life totally on your own when you can be connected to God and have His touch upon you?

Prosperity Is Love

Some have said, "You ought to teach more on love." I respond by telling them, "God is love—and so is His prosperity."

Most marital fights are over money. In my years of counseling, I've never had a couple come into my office and say, "Our problem is we have too much money!"

If you are married and have children, you must clothe and feed them, which becomes more expensive each passing year. Add a private education and the costs skyrocket.

It was John, called by biblical scholars "the apostle of love," who wished that we may prosper and be in health even as our soul prospers (3 John 2). The word *prosper* used here is a Jewish concept from the Hebrew word, "shalom." It doesn't just mean "peace" or "prosperity"—*shalom* encompasses our "total well being in this life."

It reminds us that Jesus declares, *"The thief cometh not, but for to steal, and to kill, and to destroy: I am come that they might have life, and that they might have it more abundantly*" (John 10:10 KJV).

Don't be Selfish With Your Faith

Financial abundance is one area where we can "exercise our faith" and never really come to an end of the matter because we can always use more, save more, and increase our giving into the Gospel of the Lord Jesus Christ.

In essence, Christians who refuse to use their faith regarding finances are the ultimate in selfishness! Why? Because they only want to use their faith for themselves—and not to touch the lives of others. Jesus gave us this commission: *"Go into all the world and preach the good news to all creation. Whoever believes and is baptized will be saved, but whoever does not believe will be condemned"* (Mark 16:15).

If you truly believe these words of Jesus, you will do everything in your power to funnel as much money into the Gospel to reach as many people as possible.

As believers, we ought to *enjoy* giving more each year into the Lord's work than we did the year before!

Blessed Beyond Measure

When my wife and I were first married we had virtually nothing—except the $400 Sue's grandfather had given to us for a wedding present. Yet we moved from Ohio to Texas to attend seminary.

I know what it's like to have a $10-a-week grocery budget for two people.

Please don't take what I about to tell you as boasting—far from it—it is a testimony of the direct result of a financial covenant we made with God. He has blessed us beyond measure. From 1976 through 2005, the first 29 years of our marriage, Sue and I have given in excess of $885,000 into the Gospel of the Lord Jesus Christ. At the time of this writing, the largest offering we have ever given to God's work is $100,000. And we don't want to stop there. I am looking forward to the time when we can sit in church and write a check for $1,000,000 for the advance of His Kingdom!

The Entry Fee

Tithing is God's admission price into His covenant of prosperity. And this ten percent does not get you in to see all the attractions—it is just the entry fee. Like Six Flags, the admission price allows you access, yet there is always a need for greater expenditure once inside. So, if you don't want to pay the fee, then please don't complain about not seeing all the sights or grumble because those who did are enjoying themselves.

You say, "I don't believe in tithing. Ten percent is too high." If this is your position, then generate the finances you can with your own strength and intelligence, but don't get upset when others are supernaturally blessed by God.

The Lord is not going to cut the admission fee into His covenant of prosperity to 5% just because you don't believe in tithing.

The Faith Line

There will never be the touch of God upon any of our lives until we dare to believe and cross the faith line of tithing. *"Do not merely listen to the word, and so deceive yourselves. Do what it says"* (James 1:22).

When people hear the Word in church or read it for themselves, then don't act upon it, they fool themselves. You say you believe the Father, but how is your faith evidenced? What have you done to show God you have taken Him at His Word? James says, *"...faith without deeds is useless"* (James 2:20), and he adds, *"...faith without deeds is dead"* (v.26).

In the first section of this book, I discussed how to walk

independently in financial covenant with God Most High. I wrote about labor, connections and partnerships. How is God able to distribute money to His people and into His Gospel? By blessing the *labor* of His people—and this is what gives us the *ability* to tithe.

Don't Play Games

As a pastor, I encounter people who play mental games with their Maker. They say, "Lord, you know I only earn $100 a week and I need all of it to balance my budget. But if You will let me make $1,000 a week, *then* I will give You the tithe."

These people forget Jesus Himself taught, *"Whoever can be trusted with very little can also be trusted with much, and whoever is dishonest with very little will also be dishonest with much. So if you have not been trustworthy in handling worldly wealth, who will trust you with true riches? And if you have not been trustworthy with someone else's property, who will give you property of your own?"* (Luke 16:10-12).

If we do not prove ourselves faithful in little things, then we are not giving God any reason or justification to bless us any further than He already has. When you first come to the Lord, He is looking for you to tangibly express your faith in Him.

God helps you by giving you a "starter kit." *"Now he who supplies seed to the sower and bread for food will also supply and increase your store of seed and will enlarge the harvest of your righteousness"* (2 Corinthians 9:10; see also Isaiah 55:10.)

Tithing is not solely under the Old Covenant or the New; it is a *principle*—a law of prosperity. Just as the moral law of God transcends testaments, so does the law of tithing—the first fruits are due Him.

Budgeting The Tithe

When people are first saved, they have typically been living on 100% of their net income. Then, when they first hear God's law of tithing, it can be a financial shock to their system—and to their budget. Consequently, for them to begin tithing, it is going to take faith and action. Most likely, they will need to cut their spending to cover the tithe. They may have to delay increases in some areas of their personal budget or even lower their monthly debt payment load.

These actions are taken so they can "afford" to give God what belongs to Him, however, they soon learn they cannot afford *not* to tithe!

If a person comes to Christ totally destitute, with no job, the Lord will still provide "seed for the sower." He will make available "seed money." Seed money is just that, because if it is not enough to meet your need, then it must be your seed!

By taking this small amount and planting it into the Gospel, God will see it and reward your faith by supplying more "seed for the sower." However, if you take your seed and consume it—then it's gone forever! In such a case you cannot count on God's help for additional "seed money." It is suppled from above to the sower, not to the consumer.

It stands to reason that if you consume everything you take in then you are not giving God a reason to bless you with more.

Philanthropy: The World's Imitation of Tithing

As a boy growing up in Detroit, we would go on school field trips where we would be shown exhibits of the great industrialists. We were taught the life stories Henry Ford, Harvey Firestone and Thomas Edison. Of course, Edison wasn't from Detroit, but his laboratory was on display in Greenfield Village in Dearborn, Michigan. Next door is The Henry Ford Museum.

Being raised in church, one thing struck me as interesting: all of these men were philanthropists. Later, I learned Andrew Carnegie and countless other noted industrialists were also great givers—and they gained in the process.

Some observers may say, "They only gave because they *had* so much." However, a great modern philanthropist, Sir John Templeton, once wrote in the New York Times, "The more we give away, the more we have left."

What are You Seeking First?

The "god" of most Americans is money—and it is also true with much of the world. So, when a man or a woman sets that first 10% aside as a tithe—a first fruit unto God—then it becomes evidence they have embraced the true and Living God. To illustrate this concept of the tithe as putting God first, consider what Jesus said in the Sermon on the Mount: *"Do not store up for yourselves treasures on earth, where moth and rust destroy, and where thieves break in and steal. But store up for yourselves treasures in heaven, where moth and rust do not destroy, and where thieves do not break in and steal. For where your treasure is, there your heart will be also"* (Matthew 6:19-21).

Over the years, there have been women upset with me because I taught their husbands to give God the first ten percent of every dollar they received. Women, if your husband is a tither, that is a spiritual and a moral safety net.

If you have a man who tithes, you have a man whose heart is set in the Kingdom of God. Jesus continues, *"No one can serve two masters. Either he will hate the one and love the other, or he will be devoted to the one and despise the other. You cannot serve both God and Money* [or Mammon]." (v.24).

What is Mammon? It is the world's organization of money and control. In other words, you cannot serve both God and this carnal system.

The Blessings Of Placing God First

People everywhere are chasing after the almighty dollar. Sadly, their pursuit often takes preeminence over morals, ethics, and even their family. However, God's plan for His people is they live such an anointed life that finances—and every other good thing—just naturally flow to them.

How do I know this to be the will of God? Keep reading the words of Jesus: *"So do not worry, saying, 'What shall we eat?' or 'What shall we drink?' or 'What shall we wear?' For the pagans run after all these things, and your heavenly Father knows that you need them. But seek first his kingdom and his righteousness, and all these things will be given to you as well"* (Matthew 6:31-33).

In Chapter 2 of this book, we read the words of Deuteronomy

28. Let me encourage you to study those promised "blessings" of God again. You will find that they not only come upon us but also *overtake* us.

What a contrast when we live a life blessed by God; we are not chasing wealth, rather, wealth is chasing us!

Just a few days ago, I was having lunch with my family at a restaurant when the manager walked over and said, "It's on the house!"

My wife and I were grateful, and laughed about the fact that twenty-five years ago when we didn't have two quarters to rub together, no one came by to cover our lunch!

It's an odd fact of life that when you really need the help, it's rarely offered. At this point, you're still in the realm of pursuing money. But as you begin to "work" the plan and promises of God, there is a dramatic change. You cease seeking finances and finances start seeking *you*. Even if you are not in need, you become a magnet for the blessings and promises of God—moving from the realm of lack into the realm of abundance.

Some believers act as though God doesn't know what is really going on in their lives. Rather than thanking and praising Him for His goodness, they turn their prayer time into a recitation of all their wants and needs. Yet, be assured, our Heavenly Father *knows* exactly what is required (Matthew 6:32).

A Flow of Finances

The philosophy of the world is "get all you can and can all you get!" We all know relatives who have money purely because they don't ever go anywhere, purchase very little and are extremely frugal. So naturally, over the course of their lives they accumulate some savings. But the people of God are to be both savers and givers—not stagnant ponds and reservoirs of abundance while others around us do without. Rather, we are to be rivers of blessing. There is to be a *flow* of finances through our lives.

America is the most generous nation on the planet, even though many times the international community gives us no credit for such generosity. Since our nation was built on a spirit of giving, is it any wonder that we are the world's most prosperous nation?

My concern, however, is that *individually*, I see people and families missing all God has for them in this realm of abundance and prosperity. The nation is blessed, the country is blessed, but what about *you*? How about *your family*?

In order to be personally favored, we simply *must* give God His due—His tenth.

The Principle Of First Fruits

To understand the law of tithing, we need to know the principle of "first fruits." It began with the first children born to Adam and Eve.

After Eve became pregnant and gave birth to first Cain, then Abel, the Bible gives a record of their lives: *"Now Abel kept flocks, and Cain worked the soil. In the course of time Cain brought some of the fruits of the soil as an offering to the Lord"* (Genesis 4:2-3).

Notice the specific wording here. It says "Cain brought *some* of the fruits of the soil..." Contrast this with what we read of his brother's offering: *"But Abel brought fat portions from some of the firstborn of his flock. The Lord looked with favor on Abel and his offering, but on Cain and his offering he did not look with favor. So Cain was very angry, and his face was downcast"* (vv.4-5).

Cain offered "some of the fruits," whereas Abel brought "fat portions from some of the firstborn" of his flock. Cain's "some" is the equivalent of placing a $5 bill in the offering each Sunday—it has no connection to the level of your blessing the previous week. "First fruits" on the other hand is bringing God the *first* of what crosses your hand.

How did God handle Cain? The Lord asked him, *"Why are you angry? Why is your face downcast? If you do what is right, will you not be accepted? But if you do not do what is right, sin is crouching at your door; it desires to have you, but you must master it"* (vv.6-7).

Are All Things Equal?

In Genesis 4 we are dealing with a truth most don't want to face—the reality that all things and all beliefs are not equal.

History makes the point clear. Even though America won the cold war, socialistic thinking seems to have actually won in our popular culture. Such a concept tells us that all religions, ideologies and people are equal. Even more, we are told all moral and ethical frameworks—or lack thereof—are also equivalent. This is nonsense!

For someone to say, "All religions are equal," is intellectually dishonest. Why? Because all religions do not produce the same results or the same quality of life.

Hardly anyone will admit there is slave trading going on in the world, yet it exists—and is almost entirely conducted in the

Mideast Islamic countries and in Communist China. So, how could any intellectually honest person claim all religions produce the same results—that all religions are "equal"?

To bring the example closer to home, in the workforce, certain employees deserve a raise and others don't. In fact, in every organization there are individuals who could be dismissed without the company feeling any adverse effects whatsoever. It is obvious each employee does not deserve the same pay.

Because of our human "conditioning" some want to believe every person is spiritually identical. While we were created equal in the eyes of God, our decision to accept or reject His Son creates a great disparity. The Bible speaks of both heaven and Hell—two separate destinations. And if all things are equivalent, why does the first third of Deuteronomy 28 list the blessings of God and the last two-thirds deal with the curses? Obviously, regarding spiritual matters, all things are not equal. This is the "rub" between the philosophies of religion and the reality of Christianity.

"The Spirit of Cain"

In looking at the world's first two children, even though Cain gave *something*, God did not consider his offering to be *equal* with what Abel presented. Next, because God accepted Abel's offering, Cain asked his brother to go out into a field. While they were there, "*Cain attacked his brother Abel and killed him*" (Genesis 4:8).

Thankfully, we are not left to wonder *why* Cain killed Abel, because the New Testament gives the explanation: *"This is the message you heard from the beginning: We should love one another. Do not be like Cain, who belonged to the evil one and murdered his brother. And why did he murder him? Because his own actions were evil and his brother's were righteous"* (1 John 3:11-12).

What we are dealing with in this story is the spirit of jealousy.

Tithing Comes First

Remember, the difference between the offerings of Cain and Abel is that Cain gave "some" and his brother gave from the "first." So tithing is the first step we must take to have the touch of God upon our lives.

Before I buy a new stereo or make the car payment, I am going to put God first financially. When I pay my bills, the first check I am going to write is that of my tithe. Before anything else, I will take care of my obligation to the Almighty.

Let me illustrate. We have a General Motors factory in our city of Arlington, Texas. Picture two men who both are hired at the GM plant at the age of 20 and purchase homes side by side. During the next 45 years the man in the first house spends every nickle he makes. However the worker in the second home—with the same number of years on the job—earns the same income and receives identical raises. They work shoulder to shoulder.

The difference is the man in the second house sets aside 10% of his income into savings for 45 years. Guess what? At the time of retirement, the first man is stuck—struggling to live off his social security. But the man who saved 10% of his income over the years is free. He can do whatever he pleases.

Let me ask this question: Why should the man who spent every nickel he ever made get upset at and judge the man who saved 10%

of his income for 45 years? To me, the same holds true with tithing!

My personal belief is this: we ought to pay God the tithe, set aside for ourselves the second 10% for investing and spend the rest as we please.

If Americans disciplined themselves to do this over the course of their adult lives, they would be financially independent. Such an individual would have all he needed in retirement and still have enough to leave a healthy inheritance to his children and grandchildren.

The "Whole" Tithe

Do you truly want to live with *The God Touch* upon your life? Then master Malachi 3.

God states, *"'Ever since the time of your forefathers you have turned away from my decrees and have not kept them. Return to me, and I will return to you,' says the Lord Almighty. 'But you ask, "How are we to return?"'"* (Malachi 3:7).

At that point, I wrote in the margin of my Bible: "in money." Because if a man is not right with his money, he is not right. And, if you are a single woman and dating, you need to realize this about men—if a man is cheap while courting you, he is *really* going to be miserly when he is married.

God answers the question, "How are we to return?" by asking, *"'Will a man rob God? Yet you rob me. But you ask, "How do we rob you?" In tithes and offerings. You are under a curse—the whole nation of you—because you are robbing me. Bring the whole tithe into the storehouse, that there may be food in my house. Test me in this,' says the Lord Almighty, 'and see if I will not throw open the floodgates of heaven and pour out so much blessing that you will not have room enough for it'"* (vv. 8-10).

How much of the tithe? The "whole" amount. The word "tithe" means "tenth," so you can't tithe 8%. You can *give* 8% but you can't tithe that percentage. Neither can you tithe 12%. If you are presenting 12% of your income to the Gospel, you are tithing the 10% and you are giving the additional 2% as an offering.

Where do we *"bring the whole tithe"? "...into the storehouse"* (v. 10). It does not say send the tithe or a part of the tithe to the televangelist, or to some orphanage in a distant land. The "storehouse" is the local church where you are fed the Word of God on a weekly basis—a place you can call if you are sick and need prayer, or to receive guidance if you're facing a decision in life.

If you do not have such a "storehouse," find one.

I have received mail from people who say, "I don't have a church like that, and this is why I watch your television ministry."

While I appreciate the compliment, I still advise them to find a church which teaches the Word of God without compromise.

There's More!

After God tells us to bring our entire tithe into the storehouse, He promises a blessing we can't even contain. He will open the floodgates to such an extent *"...you will not have room enough for it"* (v.10).

There is not a person reading this book, including myself, who has reached this level of abundance. You see, if we can contain the blessings God has sent to us so far, then we have not even *begun* to walk in Malachi 3:10. No matter how blessed you may be, God always has more!

It is not His will for you to scrape by or be dependent on a government check. He is anxious to respond to your financial covenant with Him by pouring out His favor.

Stay "Tuned In"

Many stop reading at verse 10, unaware that the best is yet to come. In the next verse, the Lord says, *"I will prevent pests from devouring your crops, and the vines in your fields will not cast their fruit"* (v.11).

What a bonus for tithing—you'll be rid of what bothers you and the fruit of your labor won't be wasted!

Rather than save money just to hand it over to the world, why not be "tuned in" to hear the voice of the Almighty and have your assets protected?

If you have the touch of God on your life, you can listen to that still small voice of the Holy Spirit when He whispers into your ear and tells you how to handle your finances. You can then be "tuned in" to the leading of the Spirit and *not* hand your wealth back over to the world.

If you follow God's law regarding tithing, He says, *"Then all the nations will call you blessed, for yours will be a delightful land"* (v.12).

I believe the Islamic terrorists are angry at America, because we have a *"delightful land."* It is also why the Palestinians are angry at the Israelis. People from the Judeo-Christian tradition are the greatest producers on the planet.

Producers Are Joyful

Keep reading Malachi 3 and you will find that by telling God their complaint, even without knowing it, the people of that day were betraying the problems hidden in their hearts. Scripture records, *"'You have said harsh things against me,' says the Lord. 'Yet you ask, "What have we said against you?" 'You have said, "It is futile to serve God. What did we gain by carrying out his requirements and going about like mourners before the Lord Almighty?"'"* (vv.13-14).

This is what many religious people do. They go to church and act sad and dejected. When they *do* give anything in an offering, they behave as if they're being robbed at gunpoint. Even when certain believers do tithe, they often get no "traction" financially because they give God what is due Him with begrudging hearts and complaining lips.

We need to listen to a man named Nehemiah, who encouraged people to rejoice in the Lord even when their circumstances were adverse. He said, *"Go your way, eat the fat, and drink the sweet, and send portions unto them for whom nothing is prepared: for this day is holy unto our Lord: neither be ye sorry; for the joy of the Lord is your strength"* (Nehemiah 8:10 KJV).

Giving money to God without joy will get you about as far with the Father as Cain who gave "some" of his harvest with a jealous eye on Abel's gift. Paul writes, *"Do everything without complaining or arguing"* (Philippians 2:14:) How much better for our actions to be bathed with faith and joy!

Tithing Produces Guilt-Free Living!

If you believe you're throwing your money away when you give the tithe, then you are. But if you believe you are planting a financial faith seed into the fertile soil of God's Gospel, this it what it will become.

We must tithe in faith and belief.

Faith says, "Just think, God allows us to keep 90% of everything we receive! All you have to do to receive more and more—and have the touch of God upon your life—is to make sure you are faithful in giving God His 10%.

When you practice tithing God's way, the remaining money you handle is guilt-free every step of the journey. Plus, you don't have to be embarrassed about your prosperity level. Why? Because all the money has been tithed upon.

Those With The Most Invested Are Always The Least Critical

Several years ago there were individuals in our church who seemed unusually inquisitive. They would call the office with questions such as, "How much are you paying for the billboards?" or "How much are you paying the youth pastor?"

When they would ask for an appointment with me to discuss the issue, I would say, "Sure, come on in. I will have the office pull your giving record so we will have it here—at the same time we answer questions about the ministry."

"My giving record?" they would protest. "What for?"

I would continue, "Because we want to know exactly how much you have invested in these ministry expenditures."

Not one time did anyone actually follow through on an office visit. They would say, "Oh I don't need that appointment, pastor."

Why would they change their tune so quickly? Because nosy people are always the ones who have the least invested. Tithers, however, know they are giving their money to the High Priest of their faith, the Lord Jesus Christ! They live with the knowledge that their tithe is blessed!

A New Distinction

I believe we are entering a day when once again you will see a clear demarcation line between those who serve God and those who do not. As God spoke through the prophet Malachi, *"And you will again see the distinction between the righteous and the wicked, between those who serve God and those who do not."* (v.18).

Yes, there is coming a time when Wall Street and Washington will be able to have a recession while the people of God—the tithers—simply choose *not* to participate!

Giving your first fruits to the Lord is your best insurance policy against an economic downturn.

Tithing is the first step to bringing *The God Touch* on your life.

Chapter Eight

The Giving of Offerings

Step number two to walking with *The God Touch* on your life involves *offerings*—gifts to God's house and into His Gospel above and beyond the tithe.

What is the difference between the two? The tithe is specifically prescribed as a set amount in the Word, whereas "offerings" involve "freewill" giving as a person is led by the Holy Spirit. In other words, an offering is given in joy and gratitude to the Lord and is not a specific amount or percentage, but the tithe is always a tenth.

The word "offering" or "offerings" is used 1,066 times in the Bible. In fact, there is so much information in the Word on this subject, if it were given the attention it deserved, a pastor would be teaching on offerings every month.

I understand some get uptight when the topic involves *their* money, including both tithes and offerings. But we must consider what the Bible says concerning achieving your goals in this life. The good news is we can all reach our objectives more assuredly with God's help than by relying on our own strength and intelligence.

When Malachi speaks of robbing God, it involves both *"tithes and offerings"* (Malachi 3:8). Those who withhold either are *"under a curse"* (v.9).

Perhaps you don't believe in such things, yet if you look at what happened in the Garden, the entire world is placed under a curse because of Adam's sin. As the apostle Paul writes, *"Christ redeemed us from the curse of the law by becoming a curse for us, for it is written: 'Cursed is everyone who is hung on a tree'"* (Galatians 3:13). (If you want to read about what is covered under "the curse of the law," study Deuteronomy 28:15-68.)

Your Escape

Have you ever experienced a time when it seemed like everything you attempted faltered instead of prospered—as if you were living under some kind of financial dark cloud?

Imagine if you lived your entire life this way? Consider someone born and raised in the Third World. They may not even know they are living in a blighted corner of the universe, enduring hardships, until one day they emigrate to Western Europe or to America and, based on what they now see, the contrast is overwhelming. It finally dawns on them: "Compared to this, I was living in a place which was cursed."

This is what it is like when *The God Touch* comes upon your life. You begin to realize, "What in the world was I doing before I came to this place of blessing?"

If it were the will of God for you and I to live under condemnation, why would He tell us how to be free—and enjoy the blessings when He opens *"the floodgates of heaven"* (Malachi 3:10)? God desires for us to set our gaze on prosperity and abundance as a goal.

Mashing The Accelerator!

My wife and I have never sought out wealth, yet by being faithful to the financial covenant we made with God, we have been abundantly blessed. Never have we attempted to operate any business aside from the ministry—we don't own rental properties or seek outside speaking honorariums.

Instead, we have tried faithfully to carry on our calling, yet have occasionally been "overtaken" by the blessings of God. A real estate gain here, a stock market profit there, and before we knew it our net worth had accumulated.

Why are offerings important? Because tithing is what turns the engine of prosperity on and offerings are what floor the accelerator!

Ready for the Word

I remember the night I was deeply touched and walked up in a public meeting and placed an offering of five thousand dollars in the hands of Fred Price, the pastor of a wonderful church in Los Angeles. Dr. Price asked me to say something and I simply said how much I *owed* him for inspiring me with the Word.

I expressed this because the first time I ever paid attention to the ministry of Dr. Price was earlier, in 1988, when we really had zero net worth. However, when we heard the Word as taught by this African-American minister, we began to act upon the principles he taught.

That year we were in desperate straits. We had just built our first church facility in Arlington, Texas, and we were under a tremendous financial strain. We had stretched every dollar to the limit and certain building materials had cost more than we planned. The bottom line was: we were behind in our payments.

The church had not been able to reimburse me for any ministry expenses for six months. There were weeks I was not paid because there just wasn't enough money. However, even though we were in this grave situation, we never mentioned it publicly.

So, at this point, I was more than ready for a strong Word and wasn't in a frame of mind to just play around with God. I was seeking a Word that worked!

Dr. Fred Price filled this need and I began to put the principles he shared from scripture into practice. Then, a few years later, I was able to place an offering of $5,000 into his hands for God's work, and literally never miss the money!

The Wrong Motive

Years ago, I tried to minister to a man who had left his wife and was living with a young woman from a wealthy family. This woman obviously didn't have any compunction living with a married man—even one who wasn't even divorced from his wife at this point. It was rather easy to conclude the gentleman had his eyes on her family's money.

When I tried to minister to him and point out the folly of his ways, he blatantly admitted, "My goal is to be a millionaire and I don't care how I get there!"

I was only twenty-five years of age at the time, but was so disturbed by what he told me, I blurted out these words: "Well, I believe, with God's help, I will be a millionaire before I am forty—and I won't have to leave my wife to do it. I believe the Lord will bless my life and I will not have to compromise my convictions."

Over the course of time, we always gave God His tenth, and beyond that also gave God "freewill" offerings as led by His Holy Spirit.

It Started With an Offering

In the summer of 1993, I purchased my first Harley Davidson. It took me six months of saving every extra dollar, but I paid cash for that motorcycle. Then, when the church was having a special offering in October 1993, Sue and I felt the leading of the Lord to give the Harley Davidson into the offering. So I liquidated the motorcycle and gave the $15,000.

Within sixty days Sue and I reaped a sixty-fold harvest which had nothing to do with the ministry. With that $900,000, I became a millionaire at the age of thirty-seven, three years earlier than I had declared as a young man!

What is important is that my financial gains didn't have anything to do with cheating on my wife or defrauding anyone. No, it was a sixty-fold harvest because of an offering.

More Harvests

God continues to be faithful and the blessings have never

ended. In the summer of 2000, Sue and I were driving west from Denver, Colorado, on I-70 when God gave me a creative idea. I acted on it and two months later my wife and I sat at a table and signed our names on a piece of paper and realized a $600,000 wealth transfer in the form of real estate equity. Again, this transaction had nothing to do with ministry, but because of this and other financial blessings, we became *multi*-millionaires at the age of forty-four. To us, this is only important because it allowed us to give more than we ever had for the cause of Christ.

The harvests from God I have mentioned didn't come all at once, but over the span of eleven years—and it was something we never really worked at. Our labor has been in the Gospel, yet what the Lord provided has been in the form of supernatural wealth transfers.

We are totally convinced our reaping is because of our faithfulness in tithes and offerings.

The Widow's Gift

I firmly believe the only way you can rob God is to steal from Him the opportunity to bless and favor your life.

In the time of Elijah the prophet, God looked down and saw a widow who was starving to death. The Lord's answer was to send a man of God who would provide the woman with an opportunity to *give*.

The Almighty certainly didn't send Elijah to run a soup line for the widow and her son. Instead, the Lord directed the prophet to the woman so she could "gift" into his life. Her offering of food opened the floodgates of heaven and poured upon her more than she could ever imagine. As the Bible records, she *"...did as Elijah had told her. So there was food every day for Elijah and for the woman and her family. For the jar of flour was not used up and the jug of oil did not run dry, in keeping with the word of the Lord spoken by Elijah"* (1 Kings 17:15-16).

Learning To Trust

It is not for me to say how *much* anyone should give. Again, offerings are to be "freewill" as led by the Holy Spirit. And we must learn to trust that divine leading.

Many times as we drive in Dallas, we come across men begging at intersections. Some are obviously disabled while others are not. But how do you know who is genuinely in need or who is just begging for a living?

I don't automatically turn my back on those seeking a handout. Rather, I depend on the leading of the Lord to direct my response. There are times when I give such people nothing; on other occasions, though, I will give $5, $10 or even $20. Once I felt led to give a man $50 because that is what the Lord told me to do.

If you are really going to have the touch of God on your life, you will need to trust the leading of His Spirit. Someone may say, "You could waste $50 if you made a mistake." However this is a mental bridge you have to cross—not a financial one.

In reality, the amount is not important, but the anointing and blessing of God upon my life means *everything* to me! Money is not my master; it has become my servant.

Offerings And Religious Hang-ups

I want you to read a few passages from the Word which give

insight into "offerings."

One of the big hang-ups people have concerning giving is they don't think it should ever be public. A second is that they don't believe offerings should be organized or planned.

This passage contradicts both of those positions. Paul says, *"There is no need for me to write to you about this service to the saints. For I know your eagerness to help, and I have been boasting about it to the Macedonians, telling them that since last year you in Achaia were ready to give; and your enthusiasm has stirred most of them to action"* (2 Corinthians 9:1-2).

The apostle writes how he was telling the Macedonians about an offering taking place among the Corinthians. Second, he was using the willingness of believers to give at Corinth as a vehicle to organize the Macedonians into action.

If one person's giving from a year earlier can be used to excite another's giving this year, it must mean it is permissible to organize offerings.

Paul continues, *"But I am sending the brothers in order that our boasting about you in this matter should not prove hollow, but that you may be ready, as I said you would be"* (v.3).

The phrase *"sending the brothers"* implies this upcoming offering is both public and planned. The real reason people don't like such offerings is because they are reluctant to present a large gift, and also don't want anyone else at church to find out how little they actually *do* give!

The Issue of Planning

As a pastor I have heard people ask (critically), "Why are we *planning* to have an offering? Why don't we just wait until we *need* one?"

To me, this is not using common sense. I am tempted to reply, "Why don't you wait until you need money before going to work?"

Paul addresses the issue as he continues, *"For if any Macedonians come with me and find you unprepared, we—not to say anything about you—would be ashamed of having been so confident. So I thought it necessary to urge the brothers to visit you in advance and finish the arrangements for the generous gift you had promised. Then it will be ready as a generous gift, not as one grudgingly given"* (vv.4-5).

Notice, Paul actually uses the words *"in advance."*

Regardless of the arena of your life, you cannot build anything of significance haphazardly. Doing great works and building outstanding organizations or structures requires premeditated thought and planning —and it is true in God's work.

An offering requires preparation. Paul told the Corinthians he was urging the brothers to pay an advance visit to *"...finish the arrangement for the generous gift you had promised..."* (v.5).

The person who doesn't believe in "pledges" or "commitments" should read these words again.

In this one passage we see three aspects of successful offerings:

1. They are known, or made public.
2. They are organized and planned.
3. You can use the giving of one to spur the giving of another.

The real reason people don't like pre-planned or public offerings is because they would rather be able to give their $5 in private. However, Paul says, *"Remember this: Whoever sows sparingly will also reap sparingly, and whoever sows generously will also reap generously"* (2 Corinthians 9:6).

The apostle believed the unthinkable—that what people possess today is the result of what they have given to God previously.

Offerings presented to God in love and gratitude yield the highest dividends.

The Envy Factor

In today's culture, there are people who covet and desire what you have, but don't want to work as you did to obtain it.

Envy is a strange phenomena. One of the doctors in our church told me how, more than once, when he has taken his wife out to dinner at an upscale restaurant, a patient will approach the table and smile, "So *this* is where my money is going."

Some people are difficult to understand. *They* didn't spend twelve extra years on their schooling. *They* didn't spend thousands of dollars every month on an education. And *they* didn't take the large financial risk to set up a medical practice, to buy all the equipment and to sign all those leases. Yet, they will act like they have a problem with their doctor eating an expensive steak!

Similarly, parents desire well-behaved children, but they don't want to do what *you* did—read Dr. James Dobson's books, correct their children or pay for private Christian school tuition.

Couples long for a happy marriage, yet they neglect to show their love and appreciation by giving their wife nice gifts or by showing respect to their husband in public.

As a minister of the Gospel, I don't apologize for the message of scripture on *any* subject, including tithing or giving offerings to God.

Ignorance Of The Word Brings Poverty

A few years ago a young couple came up to greet my wife and I after a Sunday morning service. The husband told us how much he enjoyed the service, then proceeded to say how he disagreed with the way we used Luke 6:38 just before we received the offering. The verse he was referring to reads, *"Give, and it will be given to you. A good measure, pressed down, shaken together and running over, will be poured into your lap. For with the measure you use, it will be measured to you."*

I couldn't believe what I was hearing. Here was this young man criticizing something he obviously knew little about. I could tell he had no comprehension of sowing and reaping.

Being polite, I listened and said nothing. However, the Bible teaches truth—and we have personally experienced abundance.

You Will Abound!

The Lord is not only concerned with *what* we give but *how*. He looks at our attitude to see if we are giving according to His Word: *"Each man should give what he has decided in his heart to give, not reluctantly or under compulsion, for God loves a cheerful giver"* (2 Corinthians 9:7).

Scripture does not say, "God loves a *tearful—or a fearful* giver." Rather, *"God loves a* <u>*cheerful*</u> *giver."*

The next verse gives us a preview of the results: *"And God is able to make all grace abound to you, so that in all things at all times, having all that you need, you will abound in every good work"* (v.8).

More Than Enough

The reason I believe you will arrive at your financial objective is because of three important words in the scripture above: *"God is able."*

In our early married years, Sue and I would personalize the verse as a prayer, saying out loud, "God is able to make all grace abound to *me*, so that in all things at all times, having all that *I* need, *I* will abound in every good work."

This is why God wants us to have *more* than enough: so we can be plentiful and abundant in every good work touched by our hearts and hands.

The Challenge

It wasn't too many years ago when Sue and I gave our one-year-old Jeep Grand Cherokee Limited into a "Challenge Offering" at the church we pastor. I had purchased the vehicle, but one Sunday a member of our congregation put his arm around me and said, "Pastor, that's not the car you should be driving."

I decided to trade the Jeep, but as I was getting ready for the transaction, the Lord impressed upon me, "You don't need the money. Give the vehicle to My work."

He was right—and I cheerfully gave the Jeep totally to Him in the offering.

Have you ever been in a church service and, touched by the Spirit, longed to give a hundred dollars, but you just didn't have the money. It's not a pleasant feeling. This is why the Lord wants you to have *more* than enough—so you can abound: *"As it is written:*

'He has scattered abroad his gifts to the poor; his righteousness endures forever.' Now he who supplies seed to the sower and bread for food will also supply and increase your store of seed and will enlarge the harvest of your righteousness" (2 Corinthians 9:9-10).

I love the next verse: *"You will be made rich in every way so that you can be generous on every occasion, and through us your generosity will result in thanksgiving to God"* (v.11).

When you have more than you need, and the Lord tells you, "Give that person twenty dollars," you are able to respond without questioning. You are so blessed you are only concerned with what you believe God desires.

Since you have the Father's overflow, if the Lord says, "Write out a check to that ministry for $1,000" you will do it with joy, because the money is not as important as obeying God.

This is how the Lord wants the body of Christ to live. Every offering is a stepping stone to a lifestyle of *more* than enough.

Chapter Nine

Diligence in Work

Prayer is *never* a substitute for work. You can fall to your knees and pray until the cows come home, but you are not going to get the cows milked or your bills paid through prayer alone.

When you study the Bible on this subject, please understand that physical labor is both *assumed* and *demanded.*

In an earlier chapter we referred to the verse which says if we don't work we won't eat, but look at the words immediately preceding this truth: *"For even when we were with you, this we commanded you, that if any would not work, neither should he eat"* (2 Thessalonians 3:10). Labor is a *command!*

Paul is not referring to the person who is disabled, or someone who lost their job last week and is now out looking for work. He is speaking of "willful unemployment"—the man or woman who *"would not work."*

Step number three in experiencing *The God Touch* is to practice diligence in the task the Lord has given us.

"Are You Working?"

The Germans have a proverb which says, "When the stomach grows empty, the head begins to think."

The problem with our welfare mentality is that if you pay people to stay home, then they have no incentive to hit the streets and search for employment. Certainly there are individuals with mental disorders or physical handicaps who need extra help, but I do not believe we should hand out money for someone to stay home and have another illegitimate baby!

Even more, I don't feel it is "Christian" to give such a *disincentive.*

On occasion we have people come to our church and ask, "Pastor, can you pay my rent?"

"Are you working?" we inquire. The answer is usually, "No."

Most people in our church work every day and never miss a car or house payment. They are "paying their own freight."

As a pastor, what am I supposed to do? Do I take the tithe money hard working members have given the church to pay the rent or the car payment of someone who refuses to work? Is that just?

Such "welfarism" has nothing to do with proclaiming the Gospel of the Lord Jesus Christ. We have an "Operating Fund," a "Missions Fund" and a "Building fund," but not a "Stay at Home and Goof Off Fund!"

Our congregation does not present their tithes and offerings so their money can be passed along to those who *refuse* to work.

A Message to the Poor

I recently was praising the Lord for His favor on our lives and asked God, "Father, why are we so blessed?"

The Holy Spirit responded, "Because you have a heart for the nations and love the poor."

Jesus—speaking about Himself—quoted the prophet Isaiah when He said, *"The Spirit of the Lord is on me, because he has anointed me to preach good news to the poor. He has sent me to proclaim freedom for the prisoners and recovery of sight for the blind, to release the oppressed, to proclaim the year of the Lord's favor"* (Luke 4:18-19)

If you were going to preach good news to impoverished people, what message would you present? Would you say, "You're doing a good job. Stay with it."? Would that be what they were longing to hear? Of course not.

The news they desire is, "Someone loves you enough to give His life for your salvation. He wants you to live the abundant life." This is what Jesus was proclaiming in His "year of the Lord's favor."

Total Well-Being

Many churches overlook those without resources. How do I know this? Because they do not teach people "without" how to become prosperous.

In our church, over thirty-eight nations are represented each Sunday, and many were poor when they first began attending. I say *were poor* because for most poverty is no longer the case. They have partnered themselves with God, the Word and the fellowship of believers, and they are "poor no more."

These people are now touched by God—not just financially, but blessed in the totality of their lives.

Please realize you can attain riches and still not know the favor of the Lord. There are millions in America who have wealth, yet their ex-spouses hate them, they are embroiled in legal tangles, or perhaps they are lying on a sick bed in a hospital. So obviously, it *is* possible to have money and *not* be blessed.

When I speak of being "blessed by God," I'm talking about total well-being in life.

Biblical prosperity concerns far more than personal gain. When John says he wants us to "prosper and be in health even as our soul prospers" (3 John 2), he is speaking of *all* areas of our lives—financial health, physical health and spiritual health.

Instant Wealth?

We have all read headlines of people losing their life savings to scam artists. Perhaps you have even been approached with a "get-rich-quick" scheme. In all of my years I have never seen one which actually worked—it's all talk!

The Bible tells us, *"All hard work brings a profit, but mere talk leads only to poverty"* (Proverbs 14:23). Plus, *"A faithful man will be richly blessed, but one eager to get rich will not go unpunished"* (Proverbs 28:20) and *"A stingy man is eager to get rich and is unaware that poverty awaits him"* (v.22).

Instant wealth is nothing more than the dreams and schemes of a lazy man who actively seeks the *avoidance* of labor! But remember, *"One who is slack in his work is brother to one who destroys"* (Proverbs 18:9)

If you allow yourself to be influenced by such an individual, *your* hopes, *your* dreams and *your* savings account will vanish like a vapor.

An organization can have fifty employees with 49 doing a great job, yet if just one is a bad apple, he can demoralize the entire company. The same is true in families. If you have five brothers and four work while one of them is a "do nothing," the shiftless brother can consume the entire "seed corn" of the other four.

By the time the family finishes paying lawyers, bail bondsmen and other wasted efforts, the inheritance which would have gone to the four working brothers will be "eaten up" by the unproductive sibling. You will experience first hand what it means to be a *"brother to one who destroys."*

In addition to the virus inflicted on the family, such a person faces an even more dire future: *"The sluggard's craving will be the death of him, because his hands refuse to work"* (Proverbs 21:25).

Serving Before Kings!

On the contrary, the Word tells us what will become of the person who puts his hand to the plow. King Solomon asks, *"Do you see a man skilled in his work? He will serve before kings; he will not serve before obscure men"* (Proverbs 22:29).

More than once, a man or woman has said to me, "Pastor, I have a good education, I'm a sharp person and I have been diligent on the job. But the company I work for just doesn't want to pay me what I'm worth."

My response is, "You don't need to worry, because the Word declares..."—and I quote the above scripture.

When you are at the place of your employment, believe God

that *as* you are dependable and *as* you are faithful, if your current company won't pay you what you're worth, then you are going to attract the attention of someone else and they will offer you an even better position.

Don't take the typical American attitude: "Well, since they're not paying me enough, I'm not going to give them a full day's work." Such a posture always backfires. Give your best effort every day—right where you are!

Keep doing your part, believing God will do His—regardless of how others treat you.

Joseph was wrongly imprisoned, yet he remained faithful. Daniel was a slave, but he was diligent. These great heros of the Old Testament did not remain discouraged because of their adverse circumstances. Instead, they applied themselves and were committed to excellence.

Advice from the Ant

We can all learn a great lesson from the behavior of the tiny ant. Solomon gives this example: *"Go to the ant, you sluggard; consider its ways and be wise! It has no commander, no overseer or ruler, yet it stores its provisions in summer and gathers its food at harvest. How long will you lie there, you sluggard? When will you get up from your sleep? A little sleep, a little slumber, a little folding of the hands to rest—and poverty will come on you like a bandit and scarcity like an armed man"* (Proverbs 6:6-11).

The word, "sluggard," is not exactly a "politically correct" term, but it is biblical!

It's quite easy to be poor—just waste your time and goof off! Solomon is speaking of people who are only industrious when their supervisor is around. This is why the writer of Proverbs says the ant *"has no commander, no overseer or ruler, yet it stores its provisions in summer and gathers its food at harvest."*

The unfortunate reality is, sadly, many of God's people are poor *because* they also happen to be bone lazy!

Give God Something to Bless

Since the Lord has promised to bless your labor *when* you work, don't go to the office begrudgingly. Be enthused—with a passion for quality.

To escape the scourge of poverty and to become a success in this life, you have to apply yourself—both to your work and to God's Word. "Applying" includes giving your employer a full day's honest labor, attending a faith-filled church, tithing to God and investing an additional 10% for your future.

By adopting these principles, we give the Lord something to work with—something to *bless*. These areas become "points of faith" in our life.

"Homeless" Or Lazy?

Contrary to what some in government would have us believe, it is the *shiftless* man who goes hungry, not the "victims of society." The Word makes this clear: *"Laziness brings on deep sleep, and the shiftless man goes hungry"* (Proverbs 19:15).

If you want to get angry as a taxpayer, walk the streets of San Francisco where there are laws protecting street people and beggars. I have never seen so many able-bodied kids begging in my entire life!

Every time Sue and I go to such a city, I am reminded of these words from the prophet Jeremiah: *"If you have raced with men on foot and they have worn you out, how can you compete with horses? If you stumble in safe country, how will you manage in the thickets by the Jordan?"* (Jeremiah 12:5).

Here, in the richest nation on the planet, there are young people who can't make it—panhandling on the streets.

It baffles me that the successful man or woman goes to work every day to *produce* a living, only to be criticized by liberal politicians as being "greedy" and "selfish." The reality is, each of us has been given the power by God to change our thinking, our work ethic and our environment. We can *improve* our lives if we so desire.

Why Bother the Lord?

Not only is there a spiritual side to success, there is a practical side.

I believe God is not going to do anything for you that you can accomplish for yourself. For example, even though I consider myself a man who walks by faith in God, the Lord has never come along and cut my grass, washed my car or shined my shoes!

The same rule applies to health. I have the ability to regulate how much food I consume each day. It is my choice to either eat correctly, in moderation, or to abuse my body and over-indulge with a diet of junk food!

Many Americans are obese, yet people are always asking us to pray for them because they need to lose more than a few pounds, or they're having hip and knee surgeries since their joints can no longer take the strain of the weight. These maladies, however, are totally self-inflicted.

Diabetes is the leading cause of blindness and amputations today in America, yet this disease can be largely regulated through diet and exercise. So, even in the area of health, Christian people too often expect God to perform what they should be doing for themselves.

Certainly there are situations not of our own making where only the Lord can intervene. This is where faith steps in. We ask the Lord to do what we cannot—and this is a proper use of prayer.

The Devil's Targets

Once a person commits his or her life to Christ, the devil has only three targets to attack:

1. Our personal relationships—especially in the home or family.
2. Our physical body and health.
3. Our finances.

If you can get the upper hand over Satan in these three areas, you will have him on the run—you then will have overcome! We have this promise in the Word: *"...for everyone born of God overcomes the world. This is the victory that has overcome the world, even our faith"* (1 John 5:4).

This is why we constantly teach on interpersonal relationships, health, healing and prosperity—they are the day to day issues every believer faces.

Your Obligation

Too many Christians live under the mistaken notion that they can rely on miracles to cover the basics of life. Take marriage for example. Some believe an "answer to prayer" will make all their marital problems disappear, but it never occurs to them to do something *practical*—like stop fighting!

In my years of ministry and pastoring, I've met people who could sing like an angel on Sunday, and then fight like Muhammad Ali on Monday. Too often, these same people come to my office for prayer and counseling with the hope everything is going to be all right in their home. The Lord is ready and willing to act—but so must we.

Success Against All Odds

We have women in our church who were abandoned by their husbands—some with two or three children to take care of. And yet these same women, with God's help, took hold of their situation, worked hard, made the necessary sacrifices and built successful lives.

As a pastor I have an unusual "overview." In the same week in which I hear a white male bemoaning the fact he can't find a job, I'll be asked to pray over an African immigrant's new five-bedroom custom brick home. At the same time I hear a woman complaining she and her husband can't manage on his $100,000-plus salary, I'll see a single mom with an ordinary job drive to church in a brand new car. Life is what you make it!

People who defy the odds remind me of what I read in Hebrews: *"But my righteous one will live by faith. And if he shrinks back, I will not be pleased with him. But we are not of those who shrink back and are destroyed, but of those who believe and are saved"* (Hebrews 10:38-39).

Such individuals have had an opportunity to *"shrink back,"* but they choose instead to *believe God*! How does the Bible explain the difference between the able-bodied beggars versus those who have succeeded against all barriers? *"Laziness brings on deep sleep, and the shiftless man goes hungry"* (Proverbs 19:15).

Thorns and Weeds

As a homeowner, I'm sure you do you best to maintain your investment by cutting your grass, trimming your shrubs and painting the trim. But what is your reaction when the neighbor next door lets the weeds grow knee-high and has trash strewn over his property? It puts a horrible feeling in the pit of your stomach to know part of your hard work is being negated by *their* negligence —and the value of your property is decreasing.

This was the observation of King Solomon, who said, *"I went past the field of the sluggard, past the vineyard of the man who lacks judgment; thorns had come up everywhere, the ground was covered with weeds, and the stone wall was in ruins. I applied my heart to what I observed and learned a lesson from what I saw: A little sleep, a little slumber, a little folding of the hands to rest—and poverty will come on you like a bandit and scarcity like an armed man"* (Proverbs 24:30-34).

Faith for Blessing

As a covenant partner with God, remember, He does not

promise to bless *some* of your work but *all!* Scripture tells us, *"Give generously to him and do so without a grudging heart; then because of this the Lord your God will bless you in all your work and in everything you put your hand to"* (Deuteronomy 15:10).

These words are *inclusive* of all your endeavors.

You have every right to believe that God will bless your efforts: Hebrews 11:6 (KJV): *"But without faith it is impossible to please him: for he that cometh to God must believe that he is, and that he is a rewarder of them that diligently seek him."* How? *Diligently!*

Faith will do what I *cannot* do. I can go to work everyday, but what if I face a financial need beyond what I can generate and produce in my work? This is where faith steps in—and God intervenes.

Create the Right Environment

As believers, we are not obligated to participate in what the world promotes. For example, if there is pettiness and conflict swirling in the workplace, we don't have to become involved.

You can create your own environment—by your choices, your associations and the goals to which you apply your heart.

The Lord has given each of us the ability and God-given right to set our own course of action. We need to be smart enough *not* to join in with the negativity which surrounds us, though we can renew our minds with God's Word and create an atmosphere for success and abundance.

I understand there can be discrimination and nepotism in the workplace, but generally speaking, the person who receives a promotion and a raise is the employee who has a strong worth ethic and has not been idle.

Over time, those who apply themselves rise to the top of the organization. As the Bible states, *"Diligent hands will rule but laziness ends in slave labor"* (Proverbs 12:24). Which one is your career goal?

You Have a Helper

You are not laboring alone. According to the Word, the Lord is our Helper. The psalmist writes, *"I lift up my eyes to the hills. Where does my help come from?* [or "Where does my helper come from?] *My help comes from the Lord, the Maker of heaven and earth"* (Psalm 121:1- 2).

The word for "help" in this passage is derived from the Hebrew word *ezer*—the same is used in Genesis 1 referring to Eve being created to be Adam's helpmate. *Ezer* refers to the Lord—our Helper.

If you count on man's help, you will be sorely disappointed, but you can always depend on the Lord.

As you enter your place of employment, remember, the job and boss are not your source—they are only channels. God is your ultimate Source!

With the Lord as your Helper and diligence as your daily practice, there is no limit to your future.

Chapter Ten

Faithfulness in Marriage

The key to success is faithfulness. It's true in virtually every aspect of life—in the home, on the job and in the house of God. In this chapter, however, I want to focus on one specific area: faithfulness in marriage. It is the fourth step to receiving *The God Touch.*

Unfailing Love

From the beginning, the Creator instituted marriage as the cornerstone of society. After placing Adam on earth, God said, *"It is not good for the man to be alone. I will make a helper suitable for him"* (Genesis 2:18).

Not only did God create Eve from Adam's rib, He united the two in permanent, holy matrimony, saying, *"For this reason a man will leave his father and mother and be united to his wife, and they will become one flesh"* (v. 24).

It was our Heavenly Father who placed the first bond of love between two individuals—and it was not designed for being loyal and steadfast for just one day or one week, rather a *lifetime* of faithfulness.

Love and fidelity don't just fall upon you like an apple dropping from a tree. This is an area in which you must make a commitment. As scripture states, *"Let love and faithfulness never leave you; bind them around your neck, write them on the tablet of your heart. Then you will win favor and a good name in the sight of God and man"* (Proverbs 3:3-4).

Too few people understand the necessity of faithfulness. It is written, *"Many a man claims to have unfailing love, but a faithful man who can find?...Love and faithfulness keep a king safe; through love his throne is made secure"* (Proverbs 20:6, 28). It is by our fidelity what we have is kept safe—our home, our job, our assets and our marriage.

From research I have seen that faithfulness not only builds a strong permanent family, but it is also an ingredient of wealth. For example, studies show the average marriage in America lasts less than ten years. However, the average millionaire in this country has been married 28 years. This should be an eye-opener regarding the role finances play in the household.

Making the Commitment

The foundation of marriage is the vow each spouse makes to the other. Scripture asks, *"Has not the Lord made them one? In flesh and spirit they are his. And why one? Because he was seeking godly offspring. So guard yourself in your spirit, and do not break faith with the wife of your youth"* (Malachi 2:15).

In practically every activity of life there are parallels to keeping our vows of marriage. For example, can you be counted on at your place of employment?

What if someone is supposed to be at work five days a week and they only show up on Tuesday and Thursday? Is such a person going to succeed? What if a farmer decides one spring he is tired of sowing? There won't be much of a harvest in September!

Don't keep committing the same mistakes over and over again or you will repeatedly pay the same price. Commit to faithfulness:

- If you have been unfaithful on the job, *change!*
- If you have been unfaithful to your personal ethics, *change!*
- If you have been unfaithful in your marriage, *change!*

Develop the character trait of reliability and consistency. Become the dependable person others around you are looking for.

Faithful—Blameless

The reality we see in the Word is that God shows Himself faithful to those who *are* faithful. I know some people chafe at this because they want to believe the Lord treats everyone the same, but according to scripture He doesn't. Speaking to God, David says, *"To the faithful you show yourself faithful, to the blameless you show yourself blameless"* (Psalm 18:25).

When Jesus Himself addressed this very issue with the people of the synagogue in His day, they became so angry that they sought to kill Him. People have a great deal invested in the concept that God treats everyone identically. The very thought that God might give someone preferential treatment implies we have a part to play in the success of our lives and religionists resist this possibility more than any other.

Here is what Jesus taught regarding this issue: *"'I assure you that there were many widows in Israel in Elijah's time, when the sky was shut for three and a half years and there was a severe famine throughout the land. Yet Elijah was not sent to any of them, but to a widow in Zarephath in the region of Sidon. And there were many in Israel with leprosy in the time of Elisha the prophet, yet not one of them was cleansed—only Naaman the Syrian.' All the people in the synagogue were furious when they heard this. They got up, drove him out of the town, and took him to the brow of the hill on which the town was built, in order to throw him down the cliff. But he walked right through the crowd and went on his way"* (Luke 4:25-30).

Individual Responsibility

There is probably no other place in the four Gospels where Jesus made people as angry as He did on this day. But exactly what is the *premise* of Jesus' illustrations? In verses 25 and 26, He says that even though there were many widows in Israel in Elijah's time who were starving, Elijah wasn't sent to any of them. No, Elijah was directed instead to a widow in Zarephath in Sidon. This implies God had a reason for Elijah to do what he did and it also implies the widows in Israel received no special treatment as the daughters of Abraham.

Similarly, Jesus says Elisha was not sent to cure any in Israel of leprosy in his day, but he did cure Naaman the Syrian. Again, the implication is that God had a reason for Elisha to do what he did and the lepers in Israel received no special treatment.

Verses 28 and 29 records that the people of the synagogue were *furious* when they heard this—they even attempted to *murder* Jesus because of His words.

People would rather think that God treats everyone evenly, because once you come to believe the Lord *rewards* people for their faith or actions, you then have to live with the concept of individual responsibility! And today's generation seems to resist this notion at all costs.

When we understand that our relationship with the Lord is based on faithfulness, we will begin to comprehend the importance of our earthly vows.

God does not bless *every* marriage; God only blesses marriages that include Him as the Head of the home. Husbands should remember, *"Houses and wealth are inherited from parents, but a prudent wife is from the Lord"* (Proverbs 19:14).

David's Story

The results of being responsible for our actions and faithful to God are undeniable.

No man in the Word of God experienced a more drastic rags-to-riches story than did David, a shepherd boy who rose to become the king of Israel. Look at David's testimony of God's deliverance: *"He reached down from on high and took hold of me; he drew me out of deep waters. He rescued me from my powerful enemy, from my foes, who were too strong for me. They confronted me in the day of my disaster, but the Lord was my support. He brought me out into a spacious place; he rescued me because he delighted in me"* (Psalm 18:16-19).

This is a psalm of praise after God had delivered him from all of his enemies. Pay particular attention to verse 19 and the reason God delivered David—"He brought me out into a spacious place; he rescued me because he delighted in me." David's actions pleased the Lord.

Some may ask, "Why should we take David's conclusion at face value?"

Well, "The proof is in the pudding." In other words, what took place in the life of David was a result of his faithfulness. Read the Word and you'll find he went from having nothing to being able to give the modern equivalent of $1.3 billion into the building fund for Solomon's Temple.

Here is the reason David was blessed: *"The Lord has dealt with me according to my righteousness; according to the cleanness of my hands he has rewarded me. For I have kept the ways of the Lord; I have not done evil by turning from my God. All his laws are before me; I have not turned away from his decrees. I have been blameless before him and have kept myself from sin"* (vv.20-23).

The Bible specifically records times when David *did* sin against God. The point of his life is not that he never made a mistake, rather he loved the Lord and kept returning to Him in both success and failure. David was consistent in his devotion—and it was worth the effort. He writes, *"The Lord has rewarded me according to my righteousness, according to the cleanness of my hands in his sight"* (v.24).

The Toll of Divorce

The Body of Christ is in desperate need of a commitment to faithfulness.

When the 1990 census was released, we learned that the divorce rate among Christians was the exact same percentage as the divorce rate of society at large in the United States. Then, when the census was taken in 2000, the number of divorced people claiming to be Christians was actually one percent higher than it was in the general population.

Is it any wonder Christians are floundering financially? You cannot hand over half your goods in a divorce settlement and expect to be wealthy. Actually, because of court battles, custody and alimony, the cost is often greater.

Vows are never made to be broken. With God's help, do everything in your power to avoid becoming a divorce statistic.

Demands and Rewards

Throughout this book you are being urged to make a covenant with God, but such a partnership includes demands. As the psalmist writes, *"All the ways of the Lord are loving and faithful for those who keep the demands of his covenant"* (Psalm 25:10).

Faithfulness in keeping the requirements of the covenant—both with God and in your marriage—will determine the outcome of your life. According to the Word, *"Marriage should be honored by all, and the marriage bed kept pure"* (Hebrews 13:4).

There's Victory Ahead

At work you probably have a personnel policy document which

regulates all manner of details—from acceptable dress to how many sick days you are allowed each year.

In marriage, too, there are rules. If you want your vows to last a lifetime, there are certain things you *must* do—and other behaviors to avoid. For example, *"Husbands, love your wives and do not be harsh with them"* (Colossians 3:19).

If there are requirements in marriage, agriculture and physical labor, why would we think there are no demands in our relationship with God? Yet, this is what our modern, liberal culture propagates. People act as if God is some kind of heavenly 911 service that they can call on in any emergency.

It's foolish for people to think they can ignore God, rob Him of His tithe, abandon His house and His Word and live an "alternative lifestyle." Then, when they are injured in an automobile accident or the doctor gives them bad news, they believe the Lord is going to treat them equally with those who have served Him steadfastly.

Remember, *"The Lord preserves the faithful, but the proud he pays back in full"* (Psalm 31:23).

There is victory ahead for those who walk in His ways: *"For the Lord gives wisdom, and from his mouth come knowledge and understanding. He holds victory in store for the upright, he is a shield to those whose walk is blameless, for he guards the course of the just and protects the way of his faithful ones"* (Proverbs 2:6-8).

Belief and Behavior

Your commitment to be faithful from this point forward is the only way past mistakes can be overcome—in any area of your life, including marriage.

Make a vow that your belief and your behavior will both be the same. This is what the apostle Paul encourages: *"Brothers, I do not consider myself yet to have taken hold of it. But one thing I do: Forgetting what is behind and straining toward what is ahead, I press on toward the goal to win the prize for which God has called me heavenward in Christ Jesus"* (Philippians 3:13-14).

Pleasing God

Successful marriages are those where each partner places the needs and desires of the other first—and the relationship is mutual. The Bible tells us, *"The wife's body does not belong to her alone but also to her husband. In the same way, the husband's body does not belong to him alone but also to his wife"*(1 Corinthians 7:4).

However, just as a spouse learns to make the other happy, we must learn to please God.

In our ministry, we come across many who have no concept of how they can bring joy and delight to the Lord. Perhaps, people were raised by parents who were impossible to please—or maybe they were taught in church that God can never be truly pleased.

Too often, the Lord is portrayed as distant, angry and disinterested in the affairs of men. In fact, much of what is preached in modern churches is not Christianity at all. It is just religion or philosophy, the kind taught in universities or seminaries where confused professors assert their own opinions, while questioning everything concerning God and His Word.

For whatever reason we have a generation who do not know this simple truth: *"...without faith it is impossible to please him"* (Hebrews 11:6 KJV).

But don't forget the rest of this powerful verse: *"for he that cometh to God must believe that he is, and that he is a rewarder of them that diligently seek him."*

There are biblical benefits to being faithful to God, to His church and to your marriage. Being faithful works—it really does!

Chapter Eleven

Faithfulness for the Sake of Your Children

If we intend to walk through life with *The God Touch,* we need to understand that the journey is not just about us—it concerns the next generation.

Since we are temporary mortals, just passing through, our purpose must be not only to experience the total well-being God has promised, but also to prepare our sons and daughters to know this same covenant.

This brings us to the fifth step: *Faithfulness for the Sake of Your Children.*

While God doesn't mind us living in abundance, He certainly does not want us to be selfish. Instead, the Lord expects us to have this mindset: "I am going to prosper for the sake of my family."

One of the names of God is "Ancient of Days." Human beings are merely temporal; our God is eternal. Hence, the Father is always looking ahead, interested in the next generation.

Life does not rotate around you and me. If you think it does, you are self-absorbed and will severely limit your potential. Since God is always mindful of tomorrow, if you are only focused on "me, myself and I," you'll never be able to walk with the touch of God upon your life.

A Source Of Pride

There is a verse in Proverbs which, at first glance, seems rather strange for the Bible to include: *"Children's children are a crown to the aged, and parents are the pride of their children"* (Proverbs 17:6).

Perhaps, we could understand it better if it read, "Children are the pride of their parents," yet in this verse it's just the opposite.

Moms and dads are supposed to be held in high esteem by sons and daughters, however, far too often parents are a source of *embarrassment* for their children!

There may be certain things we are tempted to do, but for the sake of our families—for the benefit of our children—we refrain. Why? Because we want to make our children proud of us.

The choice to walk circumspectly is not only so we can be an example to our family, it is also to keep a clear conscience before the Almighty. The apostle Paul says, *"...I strive always to keep my conscience clear before God and man"* (Acts 24:16).

There are hundreds of books written on the subject of how to discipline children, yet what is truly needed is for parents to build discipline into their *own* lives.

"Sins of the Fathers"

God's blessings for your faithfulness extend far past the span of your life. They are handed down into the lives of your children, their children and beyond.

When the Almighty delivered the Ten Commandments, He gave this warning concerning idols, *"You shall not bow down to them or worship them; for I, the Lord your God, am a jealous God, punishing the children for the sin of the fathers to the third and fourth generation of those who hate me"* (Exodus 20:5)

Wow! That's a scary thought! To think God would *pass down* punishment to the third and fourth generation for displeasing Him. From this scripture some might conclude you can never please God, but in the next verse the Lord promises He will be *"...showing love to a thousand generations of those who love me and keep my commandments"* (v.6).

Whose Fault?

If you have ever clicked the TV remote to syndicated talk shows which focus on family conflict, you can readily see how some parents have turned their children into low-life basket cases! Many of these poor souls are simply the seed of the unregenerate. When you listen to their stories of how they were raised, your heart goes out to them as you realize that they hardly had a chance for success in life.

Whether it is alcoholism, drug use or incest, the sins of their fathers have been visited upon them—it seems they are living under some kind of family curse.

The FBI has published statistics showing most child abusers

were themselves abused as children—and almost all serial killers have issues with their mothers. These iniquities are generational, but thank God, for the person who keeps His commandments, this curse can be broken.

God has given each of us the power of free will—to turn our lives around.

Forgiveness, Yet Punishment

Religionists have long painted God as an angry law-giver, seeking to punish. Yet, here is how God describes Himself to Moses: *"Then the Lord came down in the cloud and stood there with him and proclaimed his name, the Lord. And he passed in front of Moses, proclaiming, 'The Lord, the Lord, the compassionate and gracious God, slow to anger, abounding in love and faithfulness, maintaining love to thousands, and forgiving wickedness, rebellion and sin. Yet he does not leave the guilty unpunished; he punishes the children and their children for the sin of the fathers to the third and fourth generation'"* (Exodus 34:5-7).

We serve a loving God, filled with compassion, Yes, He forgives our sin, however, He does not leave the guilty unpunished.

Where is the Love?

Over the course of more than three decades of ministry, I am still amazed that there are parents who actually hate their children.

I recently had lunch with a businessman who shared with me the day it dawned on him his parents never really loved him. He told me, "I never felt a true, family bond of love until I gave my life to the Lord and came into the Body of Christ and the fellowship of believers."

His story is all too typical. When parents place their own hopes and cravings ahead of their children, it is a sign of hatred.

Far too often we have read tragic news stories of women killing their own children because they wanted to date a man who didn't want kids hanging around. Or, we hear the account of a woman who let her live-in boyfriend sexually abuse her son or daughter, simply because the mother didn't want to be alone.

Some single moms attend church every Sunday, yet they think nothing of having a man share their home or apartment for a few weeks. And when that scoundrel leaves, a new one moves in. I think, "How could a woman place herself ahead of her children if she truly loved them?"

Judgment day is coming. Remember, God says, "*...he does not leave the guilty unpunished...*" (Exodus 34:7).

It's not only women who have this selfish problem. I never cease to be amazed at men who attend church and put on a spiritual "front." Then, out of the blue one day they decide their wife is just not "enough" for them anymore and they start an affair with a woman in the workplace. They move out, abandon their family and move on to their so-called "greener pasture."

All the while the wife and the children are left heartbroken and confused, trying to analyze what *they* did to make the husband and father leave. When I see this happen, I want to grab the man by the ears and yell, "Don't you love your kids at all?"

It's Not About You!

The source of all sin is selfishness.

Let me repeat, life does not orbit exclusively around *you*—how you feel or what you want. What good is it to have your own way if your children grow to resent you?

Whether you are a man or woman, your existence is truly about the next generation. Our behavior and the choices we make should be guided by the impact our actions will have upon our offspring. We should each desire to live the kind of life where we can pray, "Lord bless me for the sake of my wife (or husband), bless me for the sake of my children, bless me for the sake of my home."

I believe that if we demonstrate behavior which is congruent with this prayer, God will indeed bless our lives and all the work of our hands.

Our goal should be to live in such a way that our children will have the protection and favor of Almighty God. Consider this promise of the Father, *"But from everlasting to everlasting the Lord's love is with those who fear him, and his righteousness with their children's children—with those who keep his covenant and remember to obey his precepts"* (Psalm 103:17-18).

What a glorious future we have!

Investing In Your Children

A problem which plagues many Christian families is that each generation is having to start over from ground zero. Why? Because we have done a poor job of passing wealth from one generation to the next. Scripture tells us, *"A good man leaves an inheritance for his children's children, but a sinner's wealth is stored up for the righteous"* (Proverbs 13:22).

How many Christians do you know who have been able to leave a meaningful inheritance? Instead, millions in the current generation scramble to secure government loans to attend college and live a lifetime on the brink of financial ruin.

Why do so many Bible-believing parents refuse to invest in their children? Again, it's pure selfishness. They'd rather drive a new car or go on a cruise. As a result, another generation is starting over from scratch.

Parents Are To Be Enablers

What do you suppose the odds would be of George W. Bush being the President of the United States if he had not been George Herbert Walker Bush's son?

To me, it seems apparent that the *reason* George W. Bush was able to attend Yale was because his parents invested in him educationally. And it seems obvious that the *reason* George W. Bush was able to run for governor of Texas—and later as President of the United States—was because his parents made the necessary investment of finances, time and self-esteem in his life.

Because of this "enabling," George W. Bush was able to pursue dreams and visions, that perhaps, he would not have been able to achieve otherwise.

This is abundantly true of many young people who are born into affluent families with names including Rockefeller, Ford, Kennedy and others. Young people from families such as these are able to pursue their dreams because they have been *enabled* to do so! And what kind of parents should be better enablers than Christian parents—who can invest not only finances, but quality time, prayer and the principles found in the Word?

Do you want to live a life filled with the touch of God? Then love your family and pour your best into your children!

Don't Lose Your "Voice"

Another reason to invest in your sons and daughters is that you don't want your grown children to ever resent you as being a selfish parent.

I certainly don't want my children to come to the conclusion that I recklessly spent money on myself rather than investing in their futures. Perhaps, this is why, in my own particular case, I go a little overboard on the side of generosity.

When my own father cut me off financially because I chose to go to a Bible college rather than pursue a career of his choosing, he lost his voice in my life.

Regardless of what happens in the future, I never want to lose *my* influence with our children.

Far too many Christians still have the perspective that when their children turn eighteen it's time to cut them loose and hope for the best. The problem with this approach is that you lose communication, build resentment and jeopardize the relationship.

Keep giving into their future so you will never lose your voice in their lives.

Incentives Are Productive

It is a little-known fact that John D. Rockefeller was a tither. When he gave his children their allowances, he always reminded them: ten per cent was to go to the church, ten percent to the bank and the rest was theirs to use as they saw fit.

This biblical training led this particular family into its heritage of generosity and service.

The blessings you transfer to your children should be done on the basis of incentive and personal responsibility. I'm not suggesting handing money to your children so it can be wasted on frivolous pursuits. Rather, use the blessings you pass on to *teach* them life lessons that they can draw on in the years ahead.

In our home we used "chore sheets" to pave the way for giving our children their weekly allowances. If they fulfilled their chores, they received their rewards. We also had a "bonus" section, a series of "bonus" chores that if completed would result in *extra* allowance for the week.

It taught them a pattern of life: "If you do your work you receive your pay. If you do *more* than what is required, life will compensate you with extra."

This is the way the world operates—and also God's law of seedtime and harvest.

My wife and I believed this methodology would prepare our children to perform with excellence in school. We always wanted them to understand that the more you put *into* life, the more you can expect to receive *from* life.

At the time, I had people say, "Pastor, you're bribing your kids."

I just smiled and replied, "Well, of course I am. And if you don't believe in bribery, why are you going to work tomorrow?"

Every employee expects to receive his or her pay—it's the incentive!

Preparation for the Real World

With such incentives, children come to understand that labor is rewarded and laziness is not. They quickly learn they'll be better off making an "A" than a "B."

Later, when your children finish school and have their first full-time job, they're going to be faced with reality. If they are diligent and go the extra mile, they will make more. If they're sluggards, they're going to earn less.

There is absolutely no advantage in your children reaching the age of eighteen or twenty-two having been sheltered to the realities of life. They may as well "wake up" while they're home, still in the protected environment of their loving parents.

If your children have not been prepared *by you* for an adult life, don't be shocked if they wind up being thrown out of college, fired or even worse!

If our goal is to preserve what we have saved for our children and our children's children, this will mean each generation needs to be trained in wealth creation and management. Otherwise, you could very well leave an inheritance for them only to have it squandered before it ever reaches its desired destination.

I trust you see the necessity of teaching your sons and daughters fiscal responsibility.

In the days when I rode my Harley-Davidson out west, I always disliked seeing those Winnebagos with bumper stickers which read, "We're Spending Our Children's Inheritance."

Every time I saw one, I thought, "There goes a selfish, old person."

I don't plan to spend my children's inheritance. Why? Because I want them to have more than I had—and my grandchildren to have even more!

"Fix These Words"

In order to have the touch of God upon our lives, we must do our part to prepare the next generation: *"Fix these words of mine in your hearts and minds; tie them as symbols on your hands and bind them on your foreheads. Teach them to your children, talking about them when you sit at home and when you walk along the road, when you lie down and when you get up"* (Deuteronomy 11:18-19).

One day in church when my son, Austin, was ministering the Word in a service, he said, "If you think the Word is strong here at church, you ought to hear it at home!"

The reason we teach our children around the dinner table as well as in the Lord's house is because of those words from Deuteronomy. You won't have your sons and daughters with you forever, and since you want them to excel, teach them *what* you can, *while* you can.

Do Your Kids a Favor

Concerning God's Words, we are told to, *"Write them on the doorframes of your houses and on your gates, so that your days and the days of your children may be many in the land that the Lord swore to give your forefathers, as many as the days that the heavens are above the earth"* (vv.20-21).

What does guiding and training your children in the Word and helping them be successful have to do with *The God Touch*? Notice that Moses says, *"so that your days and the days of your children may be many."* If you do what is right, the Lord promises that both you and your children will live longer. You have His

Word on the matter!

It stands to reason if your sons or daughters never smoke or take drugs, become hooked on alcohol or are sexually promiscuous, then their lives will be extended.

So when you train your children in the precepts of the Word, you are doing them a great favor.

One of the best ways to build wisdom into your life and into the lives of your family is through the Book of Proverbs. Read a few verses each day when your children are young. Meditate on this "wisdom literature" and encourage them to apply the principles.

When they are older, encourage them (even bribe them if need be) to read one chapter in Proverbs each day. So the first day of every month, read chapter one, etc. It works perfectly since Proverbs has 31 chapters. I have read one chapter in Proverbs each day for about 25 years or so. It has made the difference in my life.

When our children got to be teenagers and made a few decisions I believed were poorly thought out, I bribed them to read a chapter in Proverbs each day. I literally never saw another foolish decision from either of my teenagers. There is practical power in God's wisdom!

The Next Generation

The reason God despises divorce is because of the harm it inflicts on children. Speaking through the prophet Malachi, God says, *"I hate divorce...and I hate a man's covering himself with violence as well as with his garment...so guard yourself in your spirit, and do not break faith"* (Malachi 2:16).

When we look at this passage in context, it is clear why the

Lord does not want parents to separate: "*...he was seeking godly offspring*" (v.15). God is always looking ahead to the next generation.

If we set aside our selfish desires and *do* what God has asked, we will be qualified to expect His touch on our lives.

Why is He so interested in godly offspring? The Lord desires for them to have influence on the culture. Remember, He is *"...not wanting anyone to perish, but everyone to come to repentance"* (2 Peter 3:9).

In a nation where media personalities have an enormously negative influence on society (because of money and "celebrity"), we can, and must, turn the situation around.

For the sake of our families, our children and the sake of America, our young people *must* be trained to be productive in life—and not forever dependent on their parents.

God is more concerned with our children than we can ever imagine. He is asking each and everyone of us, "What are you doing to shape the lives of the next generation?"

Chapter Twelve

Removing Toxic People From Your Life

Just as the world is filled with a wide variety of plant life—from exotic tropical flowers to thorn-covered weeds—there are likewise all types of individuals.

If you genuinely desire for your life to be fruitful and productive, it's time to take step number six on the road to *The God Touch*, and remove toxic people from your life.

Cooperate With the Plan

Christianity is so often misrepresented. A kind and loving God is blamed for wars, car wrecks and cancers. But when you actually study the Word, you discover the Lord only has *good* in store for us. He has no plans to make us sick or poverty stricken. How do we know this? Because God has declared, *"For I know the plans I have for you...plans to prosper you and not to harm you, plans to give you hope and a future"* (Jeremiah 29:11).

The Creator wants to bless your time here on earth, but you've got to cooperate with the plan.

If you were ill and overweight and visited a doctor concerning your health problems, he probably would give you a list of eight or ten things to improve your condition. However, it is the degree to which you *cooperate* with his suggestions which determines the results you will experience.

Six Common-Sense Guidelines

In this chapter we focus on surrounding yourself with the right friends—the importance of guarding your associations. Leading up to the topic, let me share from the Word these common-sense guidelines for avoiding heartache.

1. Study the Word.

The principles of stress-free, triumphant living are all found in scripture. Yet we must open the pages and digest what our Heavenly Father has written. The Bible says, *"Study to show thyself approved unto God, a workman that needeth not to be ashamed, rightly dividing the word of truth"* (2 Timothy 2:15 KJV).

Don't just read the Word, *study* it!

2. Renew your mind daily.

You become what you think about on a consistent basis—and each day, as you study the Word, focus your thoughts on things above.

Follow Paul's counsel: *"Therefore, I urge you, brothers, in view of God's mercy, to offer your bodies as living sacrifices, holy and pleasing to God—-this is your spiritual act of worship. Do not conform any longer to the pattern of this world, but be transformed by the renewing of your mind. Then you will be able to test and approve what God's will is—his good, pleasing and perfect will"* (Romans 12:1-2).

Thinking "God thoughts" will allow you to break free from the world's grip on your mind.

3. Keep a tight rein on your tongue.

You can avoid much self-inflicted misery by carefully guarding the words you speak. As James writes, *"If anyone considers himself religious and yet does not keep a tight rein on his tongue, he deceives himself and his religion is worthless"* (James 1:26).

Make it a personal habit to listen to far more than you speak.

4. Guard you hearing.

This verse has always fascinated me: Jesus says, *"Therefore consider carefully how you listen. Whoever has will be given more; whoever does not have, even what he thinks he has will be taken from him"* (Luke 8:18).

Since this book is about abundance, it is vital to know there is a prerequisite to being *"given more."* What is it? In the words of the Master, *"...consider how you listen."*

5. Guard your heart.

There can only be one "first place" in your life—something to which you give your highest priority. Since redemption involves a transformation on the inside, The Word tells us, *"Above all else, guard your heart, for it is the wellspring of life"* (Proverbs 4:23). The King James Version reads, *"...for out of it are the issues of life."*

6. Guard your associations.

The Bible teaches us to be discriminating in our friendships. It is an exhortation too few Christians follow. Paul warns, *"Do not be misled: 'Bad company corrupts good character'"* (1 Corinthians 15:33).

Notice it does not say "good company redeems bad character." Clearly, we are influenced by the company we keep.

Wrong "Friends"

Both good and bad come into our lives through associations and environment. Let's start with the "minus" side.

It is through the influence of so-called "friends" that young people become addicted to drugs, get involved in promiscuity and contract sexually transmitted diseases. It is also how married people are trapped by inappropriate relationships which lead to the break up of their homes and families.

The outcome of your life will be largely determined by the people with whom you choose to associate—and the places you decide to spend your time.

After counseling hundreds of adults and teens, when it comes to questionable relationships, people are always quick to make excuses. They say, "That's my mother you're talking about," or "He is my best friend," or "She's helping me," or "They didn't mean any harm by what they said."

Centuries ago, God saw through these feeble defenses and

spoke through the prophet Amos, *"Do two walk together unless they have agreed to do so?"* (Amos 3:3).

As a result, it is impossible for you to associate with a gossip without you *being* a gossip. Likewise, you can't spend your time with a vulgar person without vulgarity becoming a part of your reputation. In street parlance, "Birds of a feather flock together."

To be perfectly blunt, if you have a foul-mouthed, negative person as your friend, this becomes who *you* are. You can clean up, dress up and attend church, yet that inner "nasty associate" will pop out. It may not rear its ugly head today, this week or this month, but it will. It's just a matter of time.

Why do I know this is true? Because two individuals don't walk together "unless they have agreed to do so."

- Husbands—be careful if your wife starts hanging around an unsaved girlfriend. Guard your home and family.
- Wives—see the red flag when your husband says, "I'm going down to the pub with the guys from work. I'm not drinking with them, it's just to make business contacts."

A Poisoned Potential

Again, people always like to justify their associations with those who are negative and destructive. However, according to the Word, what kind of person would choose such an alliance? *"A wicked man listens to evil lips; a liar pays attention to a malicious tongue"* (Proverbs 17:4).

If you're paying attention to harmful gossip, what does that make you? According to the Word, "a liar"!

My wife and I decided long ago to *not* allow anyone to poison our potential.

A Permanent Record

When Sue and I were in high school, there were some students who one day ditched class and went to the mall. They were spotted by a truant officer, who had "probable cause" to search the car they were riding in.

To shorten the story, there was cache of marijuana in the glove compartment. The word around high school was, "The marijuana belonged to the fellow who owned the car, and the others were innocent and didn't know about the drugs."

Yet all the students were arrested—and have permanent police records.

As Solomon wrote, *"He who walks with the wise grows wise, but a companion of fools suffers harm"* (Proverbs 13:20).

The reality is, you don't even have to be guilty—just be in the wrong place at the wrong time with the wrong friends!

Some may say, "You are judging."

I am simply asking you to be prudent and discriminating in your fellowship. Even law enforcement agencies understand this. When a felon is released from prison on parole, that person is prohibited from associating with other known felons. Why? Because experience has shown that when two or more felons "hang out" with each other, they typically end up committing more crimes together.

You're In Control

Now here's the good news. You can't change how tall you are, your fingerprints or your nationality, but you *do* have absolute control over your associations and your environment.

I've been in the ministry long enough not to believe everything people tell me at face value. No one's going to convince me their "best buddy" is a dope head and they're not—or their best girlfriend is a Friday night single's bar hopper, but not them!

To know the real you, I just need to meet your close associates.

It's amazing to me how many hours people carve out to be with their questionable "friends." After I spend time with my wife and children, and perform the duties required by my work, I simply don't have an interest in hanging out with people who might jeopardize my reputation.

This discussion takes us back to why so many are in economic ruin. If you are doing what is right, working hard and taking care of your family, the "leak" in your financial boat will be plugged.

Choose Your Friends Wisely

Your friendships and your associations will ultimately affect your future success. The apostle Paul counsels the believers at Corinth, *"I have written you in my letter not to associate with sexually immoral people—not at all meaning the people of this world who are immoral, or the greedy and swindlers, or idolaters. In that case you would have to leave this world"* (1 Corinthians 5:9-10).

Paul is not saying, "Don't go to work because there are immoral people there." If you made up your mind to never set foot in the same room with a sinner, you would probably never go to work! But this is not Paul's message. He is simply telling us *"not to associate" with the wrong people.*

Association is a matter of *choice*. Now look at the wording of the next verse, *"But now I am writing you that you must not associate with anyone who calls himself a brother but is sexually immoral or greedy, an idolater or a slanderer, a drunkard or a swindler. With such a man do not even eat"* (v.11).

Bad Apples?

If you possess a basket of apples and one is bad, you remove it. If not, the contamination of the bad apple will spread to the good ones and ruin them. The same is true with oranges or peaches.

Have you ever wondered why this never works in reverse? Why don't the good apples "cure" the rotten one? In nature it doesn't work that way. How is it that otherwise smart people think nothing of allowing their impressionable children to keep company with the wrong crowd, and adults waste hours with those whose only record is one of failure.

Apparently, they don't seem to understand the hidden dangers of associations. I believe this is because they make *emotional* rather than *rational* decisions.

The "Dissemblers"

Pay close attention to the words of the psalmist. He writes, *"Examine me, O Lord, and prove me; try my reins and my heart. For thy lovingkindness is before mine eyes: and I have walked in thy truth. I have not sat with vain persons, neither will I go in with dissemblers"* (Psalm 26:2-4 KJV).

What does David mean by the word, "dissemblers"? He is speaking of those with a wicked mouth and a false appearance.

David continues, *"I have hated the congregation of evildoers; and will not sit with the wicked"* (v.5).

In ancient times it was impossible to listen to people without sitting with them—there were no cell phones or email. So, in his own way, David made the decision to avoid the toxic people of his day.

Stirring up Trouble

My wife and I listened to a woman in the church who asked us to pray because she was "believing God for just the right husband." Then she spelled out the "faith list" of all the wonderful character attributes she was looking for in a future spouse.

A few months later, the woman was no longer attending church. We heard she had a boyfriend. When she finally paid a visit, we saw pregnant evidence of physical relations on her body, but no evidence of marriage on her finger!

If you're not supposed to "sit with them," you're also not supposed to lie with them!

Notice, the wicked have *"congregations"* (v.5). For this reason, when a trouble-maker is discovered in our midst, we instantly begin to look around at the people who surround them. Because whatever trouble is stirred up, they're usually in it together!

David declares, *"I will wash mine hands in innocency: so will I compass thine altar, O Lord: That I may publish with the voice of thanksgiving, and tell of all thy wondrous works. Lord, I have loved the habitation of thy house, and the place where thine honour dwelleth. Gather not my soul with sinners, nor my life with bloody men: In whose hands is mischief, and their right hand is full of bribes. But as for me, I will walk in mine integrity: redeem me, and be merciful unto me. My foot standeth in an even place: in the congregations will I bless the Lord"* (Psalm 26:6-12 KJV).

Success is not a matter of *chance,* it is a matter of *choice!*

Why Change?

Please understand, no matter who you are, there are always those who will try to change you. If you are in desperate need of help, perhaps their counsel will be just what you need. However, if you have your act together, turn a deaf ear.

For example, if you are living for Christ, happily married, your children love and respect you, and you are in the top 10% of all earners in America, should you allow people to put pressure on you to change? Probably not. But it is human nature for one person to exert his or her influence over another.

As you progress in God's abundance, some will *still* try to convert you to their pessimistic way of thinking—to literally talk you out of blessings!

Be careful who you listen to. The Bible says, *"A false witness will perish, and whoever listens to him will be destroyed forever"* (Proverbs 21:28). Not only will the trouble-maker whither away, but whoever *listens* to that false witness *"will be destroyed forever."*

Without seeking the Lord's guidance and paying careful attention to your associations, you run the risk of derailing your future. This is why I am imploring you to remove toxic people from your life.

CHAPTER THIRTEEN

FIND A PATTERN WORTH EMULATING —THEN BE TRUE TO IT

I can remember looking at an aerial photograph of a golf course where you could still see the indentations in the earth where countless wagons had rolled past on the old Oregon Trail. More than a hundred years had gone by, yet the evidence of the great migration remained.

An Embedded "Stamp"

In life we find a wide variety of patterns—evidenced in family, religion and culture. For example, Hindus in India will not eat beef, even when they are starving. You may say, "That doesn't make any sense." Of course not, yet they have chosen to conform to a religious pattern and the cow is considered sacred.

The average person rarely breaks free from the "stamp" which has been imprinted on their life. This is why most alcoholics were raised in a family of alcohol abuse and most child abusers were themselves abused as children.

However, if we can be impacted by *bad* habits we can also be affected by *good* patterns. Since we have a choice, why not choose what is beneficial? This is what we will discover as we examine the seventh step leading toward *The God Touch*, to *find a pattern worth emulating—then be true to it.*

The Roadblock to Achievement

Americans have a heritage of rebellion and, as a result, we tend to chafe at the very concept of following an established blueprint for success. The desire to do things "my way" is built into our psyche—often to the detriment of our future.

Personally, I believe the biggest roadblock to individual achievement is a refusal to follow successful leadership. We need to pay attention to the words of Paul when he says, *"Join with others in following my example, brothers, and take note of those who live according to the pattern we gave you"* (Philippians 3:17).

This one verse gives us four insights regarding the apostle's perspective on success:

1. Paul says there *is* a pattern to live by.
2. The very fact he refers to such a lifestyle to imitate, means it must be a *right* pattern for abundant living.
3. Paul is encouraging the Philippians to *follow* his example.
4. He instructs the believers to *"take note"* of their brothers and sisters who actually followed his

advice—that it was acceptable for Christians to live with their eyes open instead of closed.

A Pattern is Required

Whether it's in the field of golf, football or medicine, to bc a dynamic leader you need a role model to inspire and emulate.

Successful golfers imitate the pros who precede them. For example, no one tries overnight to invent a brand new golf swing; it would be futile. Instead, we want to duplicate the techniques which have worked for the golfers who have won the Masters or the U.S. Open.

Winning football coaches study the methods of those who have led past teams to championships. Acclaimed surgeons strive to build on the techniques of the pioneers in medicine.

To be a loser requires absolutely no study, thought or effort, but you must exert your time, energy and go "out of your way" to triumph.

A Strange View of Faith

I find it ironic that in matters of faith, many turn to failures for leadership. For example, some congregations will purposefully choose a poor, *weak* preacher—one easily manipulated by others. They want a minister who drives a car less expensive than theirs and lives in less of a house than their own.

What a strange view of faith!

Don't they realize that the messages they hear every Sunday will have an impact on their own success? It seems like they never even stop to contemplate the possibility they are not only hearing the *message*, but are imbibing the *spirit* of that particular minister.

The Path to Success

At the start of this chapter, I made reference to the wagon wheel ruts on the old Oregon Trail. Why would thousands faithfully follow the same route during the Nineteenth Century? Because they wanted to get to Oregon! They weren't trying to reach Mississippi or Arizona.

It baffles me when I meet individuals who want to succeed, yet refuse to imitate someone who is already an achiever. They don't want to copy the person who has already "been there and done that."

When it comes to Christianity and faith, some have a built-in bias. Instead of looking for a solid, proven pattern to follow, they would rather invent their own "Oregon Trail."

Finding The Best

I remember reading the story of Ben Hogan the great golfing pro. No matter how well Hogan played or how many tournaments he won, he went out to the driving range at Colonial Country Club in Fort Worth, Texas, every day he was in the city.

Why would this great golfing legend practice his golf swing practically every day of his life? Because he never lost the desire to improve!

As a pastor, I can tell you that becoming a successful father, mother, business person, investor and a victorious Christian will require exactly the same discipline Ben Hogan demonstrated on the driving range years ago.

Unfortunately, many believers are always looking for "something for nothing"—the *easy* way out! They will tell you, "I'm believing God for a miracle," but if Christians spent as much effort working, saving money and developing a plan for success, they wouldn't need nearly so many "miracles"!

Moments for the Miraculous

In the first section of this book we examined the life of Abraham. God visited with him several times over the course of a few chapters—yet when you consider the time span involved, you discover it was only on rare occasions when Abraham received a visitation from God.

The same thing is true of Moses and David—these mighty men did not experience the miraculous every day. Yes, there will be moments of monumental blessing, however, the Creator intends for us to work diligently—*"In the sweat of thy face shalt thou eat bread, till thou return unto the ground"* (Genesis 3:19 KJV).

Willful Unbelievers

When people turn their back on successful leadership, shun sound advice, will not listen to wise elders and refuse to be convinced of the veracity of the Word of God, they are, in effect, *willful unbelievers.*

Those who fail to overcome the natural human tendency toward rebellion will pay a high price—in their health, home, finances and spiritual life. Even worse, their children will suffer because they imitate these same negative and destructive lifestyle patterns demonstrated by their parents.

Unless these same children are exposed to the kind of teaching found in this book, they will likely never be set free from the harmful example of their parents.

There is a price to be paid for rebellion!

Ignorance Becomes Bondage

What a joy to encourage and let you know it is possible to start over. You can stop the harm inflicted by the mistakes of others and step up to a new level of living.

With God's help, the right information, plus the tenacity to act on such knowledge, you can succeed—regardless of what opposition you may face from friends, co-workers and relatives.

Perhaps, you grew up in a home with an impoverished, "not enough" attitude. You can break out of such a mentality.

Some people have come out of a family heritage where there is a built-in prejudice for ignorance, or for remaining in the lower middle class, or living on government assistance. If this is where you are *from* and you don't snap these chains, you will be bound by them the rest of your years.

What will be the result? Adverse circumstances will continue to be manifest.

Follow the Good

Perhaps your mother and father did not have perfect parenting skills—doing some things right and others wrong. Well, I believe you have the choice to follow the good and toss out the bad, and the God-given ability to discern the difference.

In doing this, you are not judging your parents or your grandparents. Perhaps they simply didn't have the same information you have. This is *your* day—it's *your* life and *your* time to choose your *own* path. After all, why should we be limited by what our mothers, fathers and or grandparents experienced?

To the best of my knowledge, I am the first person on either side of our family to earn a college degree. But I didn't stop there.

I earned a master's degree and a doctorate. I was "breaking out," "stepping up" and doing my part to take my generation to an entirely new and *higher* level.

A New Course

In the same verse which speaks of being *"transformed by the renewing of your mind,"* Paul writes, *"Do not conform any longer to the pattern of this world..."* (Romans 12:2).

The apostle was urging the believers at Rome to break way from their old, worldly routines, because it is God's will!

How does this happen? The ability to be free is made possible by God's gift to you—your own free will. The Almighty has given you the power to choose your own destiny.

You don't have to remain bogged down in someone else's "rut." Another road is available and you can literally set a new course for your future.

Make Decisions For Yourself

To escape from a negative or destructive habit, you can seek advice and counsel, but in the final analysis, it is just *you*—with God's help—who will make the decision.

If it is in the area of finances, *only you* can decide you will do what it takes to be "poor no more." If you are overweight and tired of carrying those excess pounds, *only you* can determine to eat healthy, to exercise daily and get your weight under control.

Whether the harmful pattern is debt, an explosive temper, abuse, alcohol or drugs, it can be broken.

Someone else can hand you a magazine article or point you to an Internet site for helpful information, yet the choice to break the cycle of negative behavior is in your hands! God has given you this awesome power.

Stay The Course

Once you make the decision to change your life in *any* area, you will be tempted to turn back every day. On the Larry King Show, an alcoholic said, "I have been clean for more than twenty years. Why? Because over the course of those years, each and every day I have made a conscious decision *not* to drink."

This man broke the cycle of alcoholism by embracing a new pattern—yet daily he had the opportunity, if not the temptation, to fall back into his old ways.

With God's help, we must make a total commitment and "stay the course."

"Taking Some Heat"

If you want *The God Touch* on your life, you are going to have to totally jettison peer pressure. This is what causes girls to become pregnant before graduating from high school, teenagers to experiment with drugs—and intelligent adults to remain in *dead* churches year after year!

What a waste! Years ago, I chose *not* to mess up my life in order to make someone else happy.

When God called me into the ministry, my family put me through a hellish time, but God forever delivered me from man-pleasing. During those pressure-filled days I came to this vital realization: there are some people you simply *cannot* make happy! You may love them, but if you cannot please them, there is no point in trying.

This matter of "taking some heat" in your pilgrimage toward success in life is much like the "leave and cleave" principle Sue and I teach in our "Successful Marriage" seminar. The Bible says, *"Therefore shall a man leave his father and mother and shall cleave unto his wife and they shall be one flesh"* (Genesis 2:24 KJV).

In order to build and enjoy a successful marriage, the man has to *leave* mom and dad and *cleave* to his new wife. If there is no *leaving*, the marriage will not work—and if there is no *cleaving*, the union will fail.

The Old Must Be Replaced

The same is true with patterns. There must be a conscious daily decision to *leave* the old destructive lifestyle habits behind, and a equally powerful decision to *cleave* to the new, positive lifestyle instead. The old must be *replaced* with the new.

Consider the words Paul writes to young Timothy: *"What you heard from me keep as the pattern of sound teaching, with faith and love in Christ Jesus"* (2 Timothy 1:13).

The reason people fail in their attempts to overcome bad habits is because of the vacuum it creates. Only when a new, positive habit fills the void of the discarded pattern, will there be a permanent, positive change.

Study the teachings of the New Testament and you'll learn if you are going to cast the devil out, be sure you are then filled with the Holy Spirit. Why? When you tell Satan to flee, you can't leave him a place to return.

Where to Find Your Pattern

Unless an individual lifts up his or her eyes to see a higher vision, the old negative cycles of family, culture and religion will perpetuate forever, across many generations.

If you are ready to embrace a new level of living, make certain that you choose one which is joy-filled and proven to be successful.

The most positive lifestyle examples you will ever find are in God's Word—from the heros of the Old Testament to the followers of Christ found in the Gospels and the epistles of Paul. And, in this generation, there are believers who have chosen to follow the Lord and are living testimonies of His teaching.

Today, it is my prayer that you will find a pattern worth emulating. When you do, make a commitment to be true to it—from here to eternity.

Chapter Fourteen

Manage Your Debt

Many fail in life because they expect someone else to do everything for them—either another person or the Lord Himself.

Here is what I have learned: God will never write out the checks to pay my bills! The responsibility for making my time on earth a success lies squarely on my shoulders. However, as I take action on what the Word teaches and do my part, there are times when the Lord *will* do for me what I *cannot* do for myself.

This brings us to a topic where you clearly have an obligation to make decisions for your future. Step number eight toward having *The God Touch* is *managing your debt.*

Slowly, but Surely

If we allow our personal debt to run rampant, two things will happen:

1. We fail to see and to receive the promise of God's Word that we are supposed to be lenders and not borrowers (Deuteronomy 15:6).
2. We submit ourselves into a never-ending pattern of living in a financial state of "not enough."

Because of a "get rich quick" mentality, many give no thought—or have no plan—to make their money grow slowly but surely. King Solomon says, *"Dishonest money dwindles away, but he who gathers money little by little makes it grow"* (Proverbs 13:11).

This is not a popular verse with those who say, "I want it now!"

The Bible actually teaches *against* the desire for instant wealth: *"A faithful man will be richly blessed, but one eager to get rich will not go unpunished"* (Proverbs 28:20).

Since the average person has never been taught the basics of how money grows, they look for financial gain in all the wrong places. Let me share this practical advice concerning wealth accumulation.

Anyone Can be a Millionaire

I am absolutely convinced anybody can become wealthy by applying some common-sense principles to his or her daily life. You may ask,"Well, if becoming rich in America is so easy, why isn't everyone a millionaire by age 65?

The answer is two-fold: (1) they don't know how to do it, or (2) they simply cannot discipline themselves to carry out a plan.

Let me give you four examples of how anyone in America can be a millionaire:

Example Number One:

In accumulating assets, money is a function of time. Let us suppose someone age 25 begins a work career making only $20,000 per year and faithfully sets aside 10% of his or her income in savings annually. Then let's assume they receive an average of a 5% raise each year during their work life.

At the historic rate of return of the Dow Jones Industrial average from the 1929 top to the 2000 top (5.25%), plus the average dividend rate for the same average over the same years (4%), this individual would have $1,485,000 in savings at age 65.

So, being a millionaire in America is no big deal—and the numbers I have given in this example are conservative.

What we're talking about is compound interest, what Baron Rothschild called "The eighth wonder of the world."

Example Number Two:

Instead of setting aside $2,000 into your Individual Retirement Account (IRA) later in life when you think you can afford it, what if you start at age 19 and only add $2,000 into your IRA for 15 years and then quit? At the average rate of return of the Dow Jones Industrial as stated above, this individual would have $1,015,000 in savings at age 65.

Example Number Three:

What if we take example two, and instead of putting $2,000 into an IRA for fifteen years starting at age 19, we invested the same

$2,000 into an IRA from age 19 through to age 65? After all, if you could "afford" the $2,000 from age 19 forward to age 33, would it not be easier to "afford" that $2,000 from age 34 through to age 65? At the average rate of return of the Dow Jones Industrial average as stated above, this individual would have $1,360,000 in savings at age 65.

Example Number Four:

This illustration is similar to the first, with one exception. Let's say a parental couple is truly doing their best to follow the admonition of the Word that a good man leaves an inheritance for his offspring (Proverbs 13:22).

If from the first year of a child's birth through age 18 (graduation from high school), the parents set aside that same $2,000 per year in a custodial account, at the average rate of return of the Dow Jones Industrial average as stated above, this individual would have $5,413,000 in savings at age 65.

Again, we are talking about the amazing power of compound interest. This is why the "old money" blue bloods grow richer and richer while the average American accumulates practically nothing.

Financial Slavery!

The rich rule over the poor through their knowledge of money and how it works. They control the world system of "mammon" to *get* you in debt and to *keep* you there.

What is their number one objective? To keep you only paying the minimum on the amount you owe—and having you remain on the wrong side of time. Remember, we said money is a function of time, both in accumulating assets and in accumulating debt. The situation is exactly what Solomon said: *"The rich rule over the poor and the borrower is servant to the lender"* (Proverbs 22:7).

The days of physical slavery in America are long over, but the days of financial slavery are still with us!

The High Cost of Interest

When I was growing up in the 1960s, 30-year home mortgages were rare. Most people had a ten-year mortgage. Then, when I was in high school, working at my father's Ford dealership, no one would have dreamed of purchasing an automobile on a five or a six year note. The payment schedule was on a 12 or 24-month contract. Only those in rough financial shape would finance a car on a 36-month note in the 1970s.

This gradual slide to extend payments on practically every purchase has not only placed people in debt, it *keeps* them there.

The only reason lenders have not successfully offered mortgages beyond 30 years is because the advantages are practically nonexistent. For example, the monthly mortgage payments on a $150,000 mortgage at 6% at 15 years are $1,265 and the interest paid over the life of the note is $77,841. But if this exact same mortgage is paid out over 30 years, the payments decrease only to $899, but the interest paid over the life of the note rises to $173,382. So, for the sake of paying $366 a month less, people are willing to throw away—out of their future net worth—$95,916!

Before interest rates fell, bankers were talking about 40-year mortgages sometime in the future. Let's look at the exact same mortgage over 40 years. The monthly payment would only drop from $899 to $825, but the interest paid over the life of the note rises to $246,154. Thus, for the sake of paying $74 a month less, people would need to be willing to throw away—out of their future net worth—an additional $72,396! And the difference in interest paid over the life of the loan over the 15 year note is an astounding $168,312! (And remember, the mortgage was only $150,000 to begin with!)

Now, just to make a ridiculous point on how the world's system of money abuses the American public, let's look at the same mortgage on a 100-year payout. In such a scenario, the payment only drops—even on a 100 year note!—to $751, but the lifetime interest adds up to $752,270! So, simply for paying $147 a month less than on the 30 year note, people would theoretically be throwing away—out of their future net worth—an additional $578,512! To me, this explains why the world's system of money promotes 30-year mortgages! Because if they pushed for any longer length, people might figure out they had been trapped by a systematic financial raping of their lives and futures.

A "Safety Margin"

Many times people at church have asked me if they should apply for a 15-year note and I tell them, "The average person should apply for a 30-year note, but pay it out on a 15-year schedule." (All you do is use a computer to tell you how much *extra* you need to pay each month to have your house paid off in 15 instead of 30 years.)

Why is this advisable? Because the "official" amount on the 30-

year note is lower, and so the average family would be better off having the "safety margin" of a lower "official" payment amount: the amount they have to pay each month in order to keep their house. Personally, I always go for safety. Then I pre-pay the note.

Saving Money On Auto Loans

Another way to minimize the amount of money wasted on interest is to consider purchasing one car at a time. The typical married couple makes two car payments.

Let's suppose one couple buys two cars for $35,000 each and finances them over five years at seven percent. And then let us assume the couple repeats this process every five years. Two new cars every five years. This way, this couple never drives a car older than five years old. From age 25 to 65, such a couple will spend $121,286 in automobile interest charges.

Alternatively, let us imagine another married couple takes a different approach. This second couple decides that they also don't want to ever drive a car older than five years, but they only want to make one car payment at a time. So what do they do? They purchase a car on a two and one-half year note. And when that car is paid off, they repeat the process. In this way they never drive a car older than five years, but they are only financing one car at a time. From age 25 to 65, such a couple will spend $52,056 in automobile interest charges.

The difference in these two examples appears to be $69,230, but the actual difference is much higher because the savings each month could be invested in an interest bearing savings account. Suppose this second couple took their monthly interest savings from only having one car payment instead of two, and put that money in an interest bearing account at only 4%. From age 25 to 65, that $52,056 in interest savings would *grow* to $170,857.

This second couple will also never drive a car older than five years, but from age 25 through 65 they will be able to save an extra $170,857 versus the average American couple.

"Carrying" Debt

Let's examine credit debt. Say you borrow $20,000 on your VISA card and make the industry standard minimum payment (which runs about 6% over the monthly interest—I looked at my own VISA cards to determine this ratio). You are likely to have a card which charges the typical 18%—the legal limit and highest ransom in many states. When I punched in these numbers, my spreadsheet actually ran out of space at 682 years! At the end of year 682 you would have paid off your $20,000 VISA loan, but you would have also paid a ransom of $333,122 in interest! Astounding isn't it? One-third of a million dollars!

You might think the example is ludicrous, but I would respond, "Oh really?" Well, how many times have *you* made only the minimum payment on your VISA, Discover, or MasterCard?

I would guess that the average person reading this book has $20,000 of credit card debt. And I would also imagine if we went back and looked at your records from one year ago, you had the same amount of credit card debt back then. In other words, people generally run up whatever debt they can service, then *don't* pay it off! They "carry" it! And that, my friend, is one of the factors which keeps Americans in financial bondage to the world's system of money!

What's Your Plan?

How do Sue and I handle credit card debt? If our car needs a set of tires and I don't have the money in the checkbook, I will put them on a VISA card. Then, when the bill arrives I will pay a fourth of it, or a third or half of it. But I will never pay less than a fourth. I also discipline myself to not put anything else on any card until those tires are paid off. This leaves room for "emergencies," but also keeps us from accumulating consumer debt.

Many people in our church "go wild" paying off their consumer debt. They will even take money out of savings to pay off all their credit cards. However, there is only one problem: unless you change your spending and debt management habits, all you are going to do is empty your savings, because 24 months later, all that credit card debt will be back—and your savings will be gone. Using all your savings to pay off all your debt is like a fat person getting liposuction. Unless they deal with their eating and exercise habits, they're just going to bulk up all over again!

Most people will always have a certain amount of debt. The point is to get your spending and debt management habits under control so that you can minimize your average monthly consumer debt levels.

If you "carry" just $20,000 of credit card debt from age 20 to age 65, you will have *wasted* $162,000 in interest. And if you added the amount owed to department stores and other special purchases, the total would likely average $50,000 in consumer debt. By "carrying" that load from age 20 to 65, you will have wasted $405,000 in interest—probably enough to purchase a vacation home on a beach for your retirement!

Financial Freedom

Some people teach that debt of any kind is a sin. How can this be true if God says, *"...you will lend to many nations but will borrow from none"* (Deuteronomy 15:5)?

Debt cannot be a sin because lending is what God wants us to do. How could the borrowing half of the equation be wrong, but not the lending?"

The lesson is this: God does not desire any of His children to be burdened by the *weight* of monetary obligations. He wants all His people to live in liberty.

Be logical, reasonable and prudent in the way you handle your money. Yes, we all want total financial freedom, and as you move toward this objective, ask God to help you manage your debt.

Chapter Fifteen

Control Your Spending

On one occasion I heard Fred Price say, "Eating makes fat and spending makes debt." And he added, "These are the only two areas in life where you can do nothing and pull ahead!"

It's true. Stop eating and your fat will disappear—and stop spending and your debt will diminish.

If you are going to have *The God Touch* on your life, you need to do your part by positioning yourself to receive all the blessings God has in store for you. This includes taking step number nine—*control your spending.*

Signposts On The Road To Success

When critics hear me speak on what the Bible says regarding giving, receiving, investing and saving, some comment, "You are making prosperity out to be the covenant."

Far from it, prosperity is simply a signpost on the road. As we have documented from the Word in previous chapters, it is God who gives us the ability to create wealth (Deuteronomy 8:18).

Prosperity is *confirmation* that you are on the right path. In contrast, if you are going broke, this should be taken as a sign you are *not* on the right road.

I could climb into my automobile today and head northwest on Highway 287 toward New Mexico. After a few hours I would see directional signs which would mention Raton (New Mexico).

Would this mean I was *in* Raton? No, it simply tells me that if I am going there, then I'm on the *right* road. But if I drive northwest up Hwy. 287 and I'm trying to get to Houston, when I see the sign which says Raton, I should be able to figure out that I'm on the *wrong* road—headed in the wrong direction. Because Raton is *not* on the way to Houston from Arlington.

Some of God's people need to figure out the signposts on the road of life! If you see one which reads, "Bankruptcy Ahead," or "Divorce Ahead," you should have enough common sense to get off that highway. Why? Because it should be a warning that you need a mid-course correction.

So it is with prosperity—a signpost on the pathway of walking in covenant with God.

The Benefit

Prosperity is also a *benefit* of the covenant.

Our ministry has over fifty-five employees, and in all these years, I have never known one of them to turn down a benefit or a perk. People don't go for a job interview and, after being offered a position, say, "I'll take the job and the salary, but I don't want any of the benefits." Instead, the average person's attitude is, "My name is Jimmie, and I'll take all you'll 'gimmie'!"

Our position should be, "If the Lord owns it, and He wants me to have it, then I want it!"

Never feel guilty about receiving something offered by the hand of God.

"Never Satisfied"

Our challenge in the United States is the constant bombardment of advertising which is meant to convince us to run right out and purchase a carload of goods which we cannot possibly live without.

Here is one billboard you will never see at the entrance to a shopping mall: *"Whoever loves money never has money enough; whoever loves wealth is never satisfied with his income. This too is meaningless. As goods increase, so do those who consume them. And what benefit are they to the owner except to feast his eyes on them?"* (Ecclesiastes 5:10-11).

The latest fads look good, but what is their real purpose?

I remember how years ago, when Sue and I first decided to get a handle on our finances, I just wouldn't go shopping. This was my way of controlling spending.

The alternative is what they call "window shopping." But have you ever noticed that, when you try it, you somehow end up spending real money?

Between the media and the merchandisers, Americans are caught in the middle. If you watch the ads on television, you want to rush out and purchase the products. And if you spend more than you earn, you soon find yourself under a mountain of debt.

Prepare for "Wealth Transfers"

One major reason to bring discipline to your spending and debt management habits is to prepare you for what I call "wealth transfers."

This occurs when someone is in trouble—which may or may not be debt-related—and their equity is transferred over to you.

At times, homes go up for sale under a judicial decree because of a divorce, or an individual is transferred to a job in another city and they *must* sell their home quickly and move. If you can keep your debt at a minimal level, you are preparing yourself to "jump" on circumstances which will bring a wealth transfer into your life. I don't know about you, but in such a situation I want to be on the *receiving* end and not on the *paying* end!

"Like That, Father!"

Let me give you an example.

In 1990, Sue and I were looking for a larger home. We would go to "open houses" on Sunday afternoons, and also had a realtor helping us in our search. Yet it seemed as if everything we looked at was more than we could afford. Sound familiar?

Then one day our son said, "I want a house where I can walk out the back door and go fishing."

That would be expensive in any state, but especially pricey in Texas because there just isn't much water.

It literally took months for Sue and me to raise our faith *up* to the level of our children. But there did come a time when all four of us were agreed on just what we were believing God for.

Then, one morning in February 1991, I was playing an early

round of golf in Fort Worth before I went about my duties. On the 17th tee box I looked across a small lake toward the backside of a large custom-built home. Since I was alone, I said out loud, "Like that, Father. I want a home like that—except in Arlington."

Immediately, in my "spirit man," I saw my car driving up a particular street back in Arlington. I knew the exact location—and that there was a lake behind the homes on one side of the road. I also knew there had been no homes for sale there.

But I was excited because I felt that the Lord had spoken to me and had given me specific instructions. So I played the 17th hole—one of my favorites on the course—skipped the 18th and did as the Holy Spirit had instructed me. Sure enough, there was a brand new property for sale that hadn't been on the market previously.

A "Ridiculous" Offer

We learned the home had been built by a bank executive for his own family. But just as construction was nearing completion, the banker was unexpectedly transferred. He listed the house, but couldn't get his price fast enough. Then the bank's relocation division purchased his house and listed it at a lower price, yet they still couldn't find a buyer.

The reason they were having trouble marketing this particular home was because it wasn't really finished—and most people can only envision what *is*—not what *can be.*

The home backed up to water—a desirable feature—but even so, there was no pool, no fence, only ugly railroad ties stair-stepped from the yard down to the lower lot which was at water level. Other items were unfinished, such as the interior cabinets with no knobs on them.

When the bank was unable to get an offer for the reduced listing, they cut the price once more. That's when Sue and I made a ridiculous bid. The bank came back to us $5,000 over "ridiculous" and we purchased the new home at nearly $150,000 under market value.

A Supernatural Increase

Later, when we sold the house, it was appraised at $175,000 over what we had paid—and even selling at a discount to help someone out, Sue and I realized a profit of $150,000. You can do that when you have more than you need!

The financial increase had nothing to do with my skill in real estate or my business acumen. No, I was led to the house—and to the ultimate profit—by God. For us, this was a *supernatural* wealth transfer!

In one afternoon, sitting at a closing table, our net worth jumped $150,000. And it was not through labor, rather by the "leading of the Holy Spirit." God can add more wealth to your bottom line in one day than you could save up in ten years after taxes and tithes!

Out of Our Bracket?

The house Sue and I live in at the time of this writing has a story too. It was built for a man at a certain price, then when his business ran into trouble, he could not close on the home. Instead, it was sold to the developer of the neighborhood.

It was the home of his dreams, but he, too, had a problem. The developer had a personal house to sell. And after quite some time of owning two homes, plus all his other business obligations, he gave in and listed the new house as well as his old house. The first to sell was the new one.

He offered the house at a $400,000 discount from the original builder's price.

When Sue and I looked around north Arlington for homes in a certain price bracket, this was not on our list—since it was quite a bit more than the dollar range we had specified to our brokers. However, when I saw the home and the lot, I told our realtors I wanted to look inside.

It was a few days before we walked through the house, and during that short interval the selling price was marked down once more by the owner this time by $200,000.

More than Pocket Change!

Sue and I made an offer and purchased our current home at a $625,000 discount from the original selling price. Another *supernatural* wealth transfer from God!

We're not talking about pocket change—and I didn't have to work the second shift at Winn-Dixie for the money. It was a gift from God—$625,000!

At the closing, everything the man owed against the house was listed—even the cleaning ladies who had to hire an attorney to file a lien on the property to get their back pay! When I added up the man's debts on the house, he barely received any money from the closing.

There is a moral to the story. The developer was so "jammed up" with debt, he found himself on the *losing* end of a wealth transfer.

The problem with most Christians is that even if they *did* receive a *supernatural* increase, they would have to give up the unexpected increase to debt. Sue and I had worked for many years to control our spending—to make certain when a wealth transfer came, it would be ours to keep.

Delight Yourself!

I grow weary of ministers constantly misrepresenting the Word, saying, "God only promised to meet your needs, not your desires."

This is simply not true. Read these words penned by David: *"Delight yourself in the Lord and he will give you the desires of your heart"* (Psalm 37:4).

If I am going to take someone's advice, I'd rather choose David, who lived the ultimate rags-to-riches story.

God's Word is the best blueprint you will ever discover for finding the strength and courage to discipline every area of your life—including how to handle finances.

By following His principles, you *will* have every desire of your heart.

CHAPTER SIXTEEN

PROSPERITY CONFESSION

The entire kingdom of God operates by the laws of reciprocity, sowing and reaping, seedtime and harvest. The implication of this is that your abundance will come to you over time. It is also why you must keep the forces of life—your faith, actions and the words which constantly come out of your mouth—all moving in the same direction.

One of these "forces of life" is the tenth step toward *The God Touch*—prosperity confession.

I am fully aware that there are many Christian ministers who teach that we ought not have anything, as if we somehow glorify God by our poverty and infirmity. However, in my own experience, I've been needy and sick—and didn't like either! Also, I could not see how the Lord was being edified through my afflictions.

Now, after applying the Word, God has given me countless opportunities to share with others His *goodness* and how it is His will for us to prosper, both in finances and health.

"How Much More"

People who are supposed to be God's children and His representatives, accuse the Lord of doing things which we put people in prison for here on earth! For example, if parents were to inject their child with cancer cells from some research laboratory, they would serve a prison term. Yet, many say it is God who causes sickness and disease.

I'm sure we can agree that God is at least as good a person as I am—and there is no way I would purposely make my own children sick! Consider these words of Jesus: *"If you, then, though you are evil, know how to give good gifts to your children, how much more will your Father in heaven give good gifts to those who ask him!"* (Matthew 7:11)

Hopefully, the Lord Jesus didn't consider His hearers to be "evil." He was making the point that in *comparison* to God, His hearers *were* evil. Yet, if such individuals knew how to give good gifts to their sons and daughters, *"how much more"* will the Lord do for those who ask?

God has no intention of harming you, only *"plans to give you hope and a future"* (Jeremiah 29:11).

Five Bold Steps

In 1989, Sue and I were flat broke. By that I mean for every asset we had, there was a corresponding liability.

At this point we received the message you are reading in this book—and crossed the faith line. Immediately, we took five bold steps:

One: We acknowledged that God, and only God, was our Source.

Two: We obeyed the Lord by saving something every seven days, both at home and in our ministry. (The reason I said "obeyed" is because God told me I didn't have anything because I didn't *save* anything—and without saving there would not be any "barns" containing crops for God to bless.)

Three: We believed God's promise to bless what we saved and whatever we put our hands to.

Four: We kept giving to God, both tithes and offerings.

Five: We made a concerted effort to renew our minds by the Word of God—to upgrade our expectations and to change our confession. We realized that in order for us to walk in abundance and prosperity, we had to discipline ourselves to say the same thing God says. At this point, Sue and I were off and running.

The Power Of The Tongue

Our culture, even our *Christian* culture, has always had a great *prejudice* against positive confession. Sure, we are familiar with the "confession" of a criminal and the "confessionals" practiced in the Roman churches, yet there is a "profession" in the New Testament which deals more with what we *want* as opposed to an admission of guilt over something we have done wrong.

In order for us to walk in the blessings of the Almighty, we must discipline ourselves to say the same thing about our lives that God says. Remember, *"Death and life are in the power of the tongue: and they that love it shall eat the fruit thereof"* (Proverbs 18:21 KJV).

It does not say "life and death," but "death and life." I believe the emphasis is placed on *death* because when you listen to most people, they speak of what is *not* enough (sickness and death) rather than confessing what is *more* than enough (life and health).

In normal conversation, you will find that what is spoken by the average human is more negative than positive. Yet the life-changing Word of God is meant to be in your mouth! As Paul writes, *"But what saith it? The word is nigh thee, even in thy mouth, and in thy heart: that is, the word of faith, which we preach"* (Romans 10:8 KJV).

In this verse the apostle refers to what Moses declared centuries earlier: *"But the word is very nigh unto thee, in thy mouth, and in thy heart, that thou mayest do it"* (Deuteronomy 30:14 KJV).

The entire point of the Word of God is for us to *believe* and do. However, in today's society, we are often trained to approach scripture as if it is the story of an ancient culture or a fairy tale.

Walking By Faith

People have a built-in opposition to confessing, believing and doing the Word. Some go so far as to say, "It doesn't make any sense."

Let me remind you, though, that as Christians we do not walk by what the world calls logic or "sense," rather by faith in the Word: *"For we walk by faith, not by sight"* (2 Corinthians 5:7 KJV).

We demonstrate this every time we act on what God says concerning our lives.

Most Christians use "faith talk," but usually only in acceptable ways. For example, you might hear a believer speak about going to heaven when they die. But how do they *know* they're going to heaven—or that there *is* even such a place? They base it on scripture.

Let me ask, "What is the difference in saying what God says *will* happen to me as a believer when I die, versus confessing what God says *should* happen to me while I'm alive?"

The only difference I can imagine is: we are afraid to confess what the Lord says should take place because if it doesn't, our "faith failure" will be exposed—everyone will see it.

We also have to fight our flesh, which wants to say only what our eyes are seeing and our bodies are feeling. Yet, we are not supposed to be walking by sight alone, rather by faith in the Word of the Lord: *"My soul finds rest in God alone; my salvation comes from him. He alone is my rock and my salvation; he is my fortress, I will never be shaken"* (Psalm 62:1).

Speak to Your Mountain

If you want to walk in abundance, I cannot overemphasize the necessity of disciplining yourself to say exactly what God says. The classic passage on confession is found in Mark 11, which records the words of Jesus on the subject: *"And Jesus answering saith unto them, Have faith in God. For verily I say unto you, That whosoever shall say unto this mountain, Be thou removed, and be thou cast into the sea; and shall not doubt in his heart, but shall believe that those things which he saith shall come to pass; he shall have whatsoever he saith. Therefore I say unto you, What things soever ye desire, when ye pray, believe that ye receive them, and ye shall have them"* (Mark 11:22-24 KJV, emphasis mine).

Notice, Jesus uses some form of the word "say" three times, and the word "believe" just once. So why do Christians spend practically all their time learning how to better believe, but spend little time learning how to better *confess?* Perhaps, we need to pay three times as much attention to what we say as what we believe.

A "Self-Fulfilling Prophecy"

The reason we need to "renew" our thinking is because our mind (reason) automatically rejects the concept that what we say has anything at all to do with what we experience in life. Our normal response is, *after* things happen to us, we talk about it. Absolutely foreign to our thinking is that we talk about events—*then* they happen.

Even though the church may not fully embrace what Jesus was saying concerning "speaking to mountains," the world has its own interpretation—and in psychology it is called a "self-fulfilling prophecy."

Here is the truth every believer needs to understand: We don't receive what we want or desire, or what is good. We don't even receive the *will* of God. Instead, *what we get is what we say!*

To walk in the power of the message Jesus was giving, we must comprehend this revolutionary concept and understand how God operates.

When Jesus said to Peter, *"...Have faith in God..."* (Mark 11:22 KJV), these words can be translated from the Greek, "Have the faith of God" or "Have the God-kind of faith."

This is the type of belief God had at creation as He was brooding over the surface of the deep. The earth was dark, formless and void, *"And God said, Let there be light: and there was light"* (Genesis 1:3 KJV).

This is God's *modus operandi*—and if we are going to have this same level of belief, it means we will have to become imitators of how God operates in *His* faith.

Total Confidence

When Jesus stood outside the tomb of Lazarus, *"...he cried with a loud voice, Lazarus, come forth"* (John 11:43 KJV).

Martha warned the Lord that her brother Lazarus had been in the tomb several days and his body was beginning to smell. As Jesus said, *"Take ye away the stone. Martha, the sister of him that was dead, saith unto him, Lord, by this time he stinketh: for he hath been dead four days"* (v.39).

Martha said what was (*"he stinketh"*), while Jesus stated what He wanted (*"Lazarus, come forth"*).

I've seen faith-oriented Christians renew their minds to this truth and subsequently begin to walk in dynamic power. Yet, a few have asked me, "Pastor, why does God receive 100% of what He says, but I don't get 100% of what I say?"

The difference is, God is God—and has total, absolute confidence that what He says will come to pass. When His Son, Jesus, walked on planet earth, He also fully believed whatever *He* said would take place.

Today, we are still working on this matter of confidence. We call it "faith"!

If we could increase our belief level to 100%, we would have amazing results. The promise of the Lord is not just to a few selected favorites, but to *all.* Jesus declares, *"...whosoever shall say..."* (Mark 11:23).

What Will You Say?

Please understand, you are not talking *about* your difficulty, rather *to* your problem. Jesus declares that whosoever shall say *"unto this mountain"* (v.23). Also notice that *when* we speak to our adversity, the Lord instructs us in *what* to say: *"...Be thou removed, and be thou cast into the sea..."* (v.23). In other words, say what you *want* to occur, not just what has been happening. This is the difference between a positive and a negative report—and how we are to prophesy good results over our lives and circumstances.

Next, we learn what will happen if we indeed have a "God kind of faith." To the person who dares to speak *to* their mountain of trouble, Jesus promises, *"...he shall have whatsoever he saith"* (v.23).

It is important to notice that the Lord does not declare, "he shall have whatsoever he wants," nor does He say, "he shall have the will of God"—or "he shall have whatever is good, upright, holy and righteous." No, the promise is, *"...he shall have whatsoever he saith."*

Since this book concerns abundance and walking with *The God Touch* upon our lives, for some, these teachings of Jesus become even more difficult to fathom and to implement.

When people come to our ministry and hear for the first time how what they *say* has everything to do with their success, it takes a while for the message to penetrate their thought process.

Is It Working?

One man commented, "Pastor, I tried what you are teaching, but faith just doesn't work for me."

I replied, "Are you praying each and every day?"

"No," he admitted.

Then I inquired, "Are you reading and studying the Word regularly?"

Again, "No."

The man offered the same answer for numerous questions: "Are you gainfully employed? Are you tithing and giving offerings into God's Gospel as led by His Spirit?"

People want the *promises* of God without having to be bothered by actually *living* for God.

To the individual who says the Word isn't working for them, I reply, "Examine your life. Make certain your believing, your actions and your confession are all unified toward the same objective."

Saying "The Same Thing"

Consider the word *homologia* from the Greek New Testament. "Homo" means "the same," and "logia" derives from the same root word as "logos," or "word." Thus, *homologia* basically means "the same word" or "to say the same thing."

This term is most often translated in the New Testament as "profession" or "confession." For example, *"Wherefore, holy brethren, partakers of the heavenly calling, consider the Apostle and High Priest of our profession, Christ Jesus"* (Hebrews 3:1). The word "profession" is *homologia.*

Literally, then, Jesus is the High Priest of "what we say"—our confession.

According to the apostle Paul, we are even *saved* through our "saying the same thing." He writes, *"That if you confess* [homologia] *with your mouth, 'Jesus is Lord,' and believe in your heart that God raised him from the dead, you will be saved. For it is with your heart that you believe and are justified, and it is with your mouth that you confess and are saved"* (Romans 10:9-10).

If it makes no difference what we say, why would the apostle tell us what to confess? Paul instructs us to confess: *"Jesus is Lord."*

Plus, we are also to *believe* something specific in order to be saved: *"...and believe in your heart that God raised him from the dead."*

Our confession and our believing must be working in tandem. And, as we saw earlier, our confession must also be operating parallel with our actions. Contrary to modern, popular denominational and "new age" thinking, our actions *do* matter! Speaking of the Jews who rejected the knowledge of Christ, Paul writes, *"They claim* [homologia] *to know God, but by their actions they deny him. They are detestable, disobedient and unfit for doing anything good"* (Titus 1:16). How did these people deny God? *"...by their actions..."*

Obedience Should Accompany Confession

Another example of *homologia* can be found as Paul speaks of how *obedience* is going to accompany your confession: *"Because of the service by which you have proved yourselves, men will praise God for the obedience that accompanies your confession of the gospel of Christ, and for your generosity in sharing with them and with everyone else"* (2 Corinthians 9:13).

Or, we can read it this way: *"...men will praise God for the obedience that accompanies your homologia of the gospel of Christ."*

When Paul writes, *"Because of the service by which you have proved yourselves..."*, he is referring to a lifestyle of actions and confession complementing rather than contradicting one another.

Paul says as much in the phrase, *"...men will praise God for the obedience that accompanies your confession of the gospel of Christ..."*

The reason others praise God when you are in obedience is because by your giving or service, people will be blessed.

The apostle is talking about true Christian faith—the kind which includes not only confession, but corresponding action.

It's for "Whoever"

Unfortunately, many Christians will *never* live in abundance because they cannot bring themselves to *believe* in living prosperously. They think it's wrong to be successful and their religion-imposed guilt trip holds them in the bondage of lack and mediocrity. Because they refuse to renew their minds to the Word, and will not "say the same thing" God says about their lives, they will never be free.

Jesus declares, *"Whoever acknowledges me before men, I will also acknowledge him before my Father in heaven. But whoever disowns me before men, I will disown him before my Father in heaven"* (Matthew 10:32-33).

The phrase, "Whoever acknowledges," is again the same Greek word defined as "saying the same thing"—identifying with the Lord Jesus Christ.

Some of the most sobering verses in the New Testament are found in the Gospel of John, speaking of the response of religious leaders to Christ. Scripture records, *"Yet at the same time many even among the leaders believed in him. But because of the Pharisees they would not confess their faith for fear they would be put out of the synagogue; for they loved praise from men more than praise from God"* (John 12:42, 43).

These men *believed* in Jesus, yet they would not *confess* Him because of their religiously based fears. They would not identify with Christ or "say the same thing," since they were afraid of being thrown out of the synagogue.

Patience And Persistence

Another reason for failure is that people often lack the "staying power" to make the Word of God work for them. They become discouraged and stop reading the Word. They become impatient and quit on God.

Let's say someone is sick and decides to believe God for their healing. How long will their faith last? Twenty minutes? Twenty days? If we operated this way in our secular labor, we would starve to death!

I believe many fail because they don't "say the same thing" or hold fast to the confession of their faith long enough.

It's practically impossible to have every good thing accomplished in a day, a month or even a year. Some tasks can require a decade or more.

Serving God and seeing His Word work on your behalf requires commitment. Paul tells Timothy, *"Fight the good fight of the faith. Take hold of the eternal life to which you were called when you made your good confession in the presence of many witnesses. In the sight of God, who gives life to everything, and of Christ Jesus, who while testifying before Pontius Pilate made the good confession, I charge you"* (1 Timothy 6:12-13).

In these verses, the "good confession" is *homologia*—"saying the same thing." Paul is encouraging us to imitate the Lord as He appeared before Pilate. At the point of this great test, Jesus stood His ground.

Continual Confession

The reason I want you to remember the word *homologia* is so each time you read "confession" or "profession" in scripture, you will remember, "I must say the same thing."

Our confession is not to be an occasional, haphazard act. It must be ongoing: *"Through Jesus, therefore, let us continually offer to God a sacrifice of praise—the fruit of lips that confess* [homologia] *his name"* (Hebrews 13:15).

The last three uses of this word in the New testament are significant:

- *"If we confess* [homologia] *our sins, he is faithful and just and will forgive us our sins and purify us from all unrighteousness"* (1 John 1:9).
- *"If anyone acknowledges* [homologia] *that Jesus is the Son of God, God lives in him and he in God"* (1 John 4:15).
- *"Many deceivers, who do not acknowledge* [homologia] *Jesus Christ as coming in the flesh, have gone out into the world. Any such person is the deceiver and the antichrist"* (2 John 1:7).

I rarely use this Greek word in my everyday vocabulary, yet I am constantly aware I need to "say the same thing" as God says about my life.

Does Jesus Agree?

Revelation 3:14 calls Jesus *"the Amen."* At this moment He is seated at the right hand of the Father, waiting for us to *say* something He can agree with, words to which He can say "Amen."

However, think of all the foolish things we utter which Jesus cannot possibly agree with—mindless phrases such as "I can't win for losing," or "The Asian flu is coming and I'll probably get sick!"

I'm sure you wouldn't like Jesus to say "Amen" to those things.

What Does God Say?

Think of what incredible things would happen if we were in the habit of declaring, "I believe God is supplying all my needs. I believe there is enough money coming into my home every seven days to meet every need and pay every bill on time." At the same moment, picture Jesus sitting at the right hand of the Father agreeing with you—saying "Amen!"

If Jesus is the High Priest of our "same word," how can He agree with us if we don't agree with Him? Can He change His Word to do so? Of course not! *"God is not a man, that he should lie; neither the son of man, that he should repent: hath he said, and shall he not do it? or hath he spoken, and shall he not make it good?"* (Numbers 23:19 KJV).

God does not deceive, neither does He flip-flop or alter His opinion: *"For I am the Lord, I change not; therefore ye sons of Jacob are not consumed"* (Malachi 3:6 KJV).

Every time you say what *you* think, or what you are *afraid* of, God is automatically going to be in disagreement with you. Yet when you say what *God* says ("say the same thing") you are in total unity with Him.

So, instead of confessing your problems and your fears, start professing what God's Word declares concerning your life.

Don't Limit the Lord

Psalm 78 relates the story of the children of Israel crossing from slavery in Egypt to their Promised Land—how they tested the Lord's mercy and patience again and again. In the account, we find these words: *"Yea, they turned back and tempted God, and limited the Holy One of Israel"* (Psalm 78:41 KJV).

Even after they heard the word by God's chosen man, Moses, and had witnessed the repeated miraculous signs, their actions *limited* what the Lord would accomplish for them.

Keep Listening!

Many don't understand the matter of making a faith confession, but according to the Word, we speak what we believe: *"It is written: 'I believed; therefore I have spoken.' With that same spirit of faith we also believe and therefore speak"* (2 Corinthians 4:13).

This is also why it is important to keep ourselves in an environment where we are constantly *hearing* the Word of God. (After all, we *hear* the Word when we *speak* the Word—with both our outer and inner ear.)

Remember, *"...faith cometh by hearing, and hearing by the word of God"* (Romans 10:17 KJV). We speak the Word because we believe the Word—then, when we hear ourselves speaking, it is of God. This also reaffirms back into our "spirit man" the truth and sureness of God's infallible Word, and even *more* faith is generated.

"Hold Fast!"

The writer of Hebrews gives this warning: *"Seeing then that we have a great high priest, that is passed into the heavens, Jesus the Son of God, let us hold fast our profession"* (Hebrews 4:14 KJV).

Such a caution to "hold fast" would not be necessary unless there was going to be a tug on the line—an attempt to pry you loose.

In a world where so much can go wrong, you don't need to be changing jobs, changing churches or constantly changing your beliefs. Instead take a firm hold on the Word of God, then hang on as if your life depends on it—because it truly does!

Again, we are told, *"Let us hold fast the profession of our faith without wavering; (for he is faithful that promised.)"* (Hebrews 10:23 KJV).

Never forget the story of Abraham, who was believing God for an heir. Scripture records, *"Without weakening in his faith, he faced the fact that his body was as good as dead—since he was about a hundred years old—and that Sarah's womb was also dead. Yet he did not waver through unbelief regarding the promise of God, but was strengthened in his faith and gave glory to God"* (Romans 4:20 KJV).

Abraham simply chose to have more confidence in what God had *said* to him than in the circumstances of his life.

"Don't Say That!"

To set our financial house in order back in 1989 and the early 1990s, Sue and I not only trimmed our expenses and cut down debt, we became fanatical concerning our confessions of faith, success and abundance. We were determined to never say anything negative, not even in jest. And if one of us slipped, the other would correct it cheerfully and positively.

One day in particular, I was in my office at home, worrying over our finances. Sue walked in and I must have made a negative comment, because I remember her saying, "Don't say that! God is going to give us so much money, we can paper the walls with it!"

Two Powerful Confessions

There is not a day that goes by without my making these two confessions from the Word:

1. *"And my God will meet all your needs according to his glorious riches in Christ Jesus"* (Philippians 4:9).

2. *"You will be made rich in every way so that you can be generous on every occasion, and through us your generosity will result in thanksgiving to God"* (2 Corinthains 9:11).

I make it my daily confession that there is enough money coming into both my home and the ministry to meet every need and pay every bill every seven days. Not only that, I confess every seven days *more* than enough is coming so we are enabled—both at home and in the ministry—to be generous on every occasion and to lend and not borrow.

This is what I have disciplined myself to expect out of life. And this is the way I act.

In my humble opinion, these two verses alone—confessed and acted upon daily—can take any Christian to a high level of abundance.

I began taking these two scriptures seriously only sixteen years ago, and during this time we have gone from lack to plenty, both in our personal lives and in our ministry.

Do you have sixteen years you can give to God and His Word—and "stay with it"?

Make your confession today!

Chapter Seventeen

Invest in Yourself Through Education

Your Heavenly Father believes in you, but in order to experience everything the Lord has planned for your future, you need to believe in yourself.

There is no more practical way to see *The God Touch* blossom in your life than with step number eleven—to invest in yourself through education.

The knowledge you sow into your future will pay ongoing dividends, year after year.

Don't Neglect the Practical

To prosper and succeed, we must pay attention to both the spiritual and pragmatic aspects of living. And I believe the most productive lifestyle is to be "in faith" while, at the same time taking care of the practical side of your daily activities.

Some emphasize the spiritual to the neglect of the practical, while others focus on the practical to the neglect of the spiritual. Even worse, there are those who totally disregard input from *any* source which might contribute to their prosperity and happiness. They are content to live with the attitude, "Whatever will be, will be."

"Lucky?"

Many Americans have become so accustomed to quick and painless gratification, they don't view schooling as productive—especially since the "pay off" may not show itself until four, six or eight years down the road.

Later, the same people who decided to forego furthering their studies, look at dentists, veterinarians and other professionals as "lucky." No, it was hard work for which they didn't receive immediate compensation. Medical doctors study for at least twelve years after high school—during which time they have very little income and practically zero spare time. Then they *arrive*, and society chooses to pay them triple, even quadruple what others earn.

All things being equal, a better education will yield more earning power on the job. For example, school teachers and other municipal workers are compensated on "pay scales" that factor education into the equation.

The one area were education doesn't seem to matter is in professional sports—yet the number of people able to earn those multi-million dollar salaries is exceedingly small. However, if you talk to an NBA star, they will let you know in a hurry how many thousands of hours they have spent honing their skills.

Self-Assurance

Have you ever noticed the self-confidence levels of highly trained, skilled professionals such as airline pilots or corporate attorneys? They possess an amazing ability to perform, even under tremendous pressure.

Surgeons are required to jump through many hoops before receiving their medical certification, and their self-esteem can seem arrogant to some—even though it is rarely the case. In truth, they are confident and *believe* in themselves.

The more you invest in *you,* the more self-assurance you will possess.

When I was working my way through Bible school, I sold cookware. Here is what I discovered: If I washed and waxed my car and my pots and pans were sparkling clean, I made more sales.

How was that possible? By going first-class and being prepared, I felt better about myself and my chances of setting records selling cookware that particular weekend!

Regardless of your chosen profession, when you invest in yourself, you are going to be knowledgeable, make fewer mistakes and move ahead with boldness and assurance.

"Diligent Hands"

Teenagers who leave high school without a plan to better themselves often take the first job they come across. They work, get married, have children and just "get by" financially.

Before they realize what has taken place, these same individuals are 40 years old and their earning power is permanently pegged at a low scale. They are entangled by circumstances created by their own inaction.

Achieving a top-notch education is not for the idle. It takes commitment and hard work, yet the results are always worth the effort. The Bible tells us, *"Lazy hands make a man poor, but diligent hands bring wealth. He who gathers crops in summer is a wise son, but he who sleeps during harvest is a disgraceful son"* (Proverbs 10:4-5).

Notice the two distinct possibilities—gathering crops in summer, or sleeping during harvest time. Each is predicated upon our approach to life, "lazy hands" versus "diligent hands."

Which would you rather have?

According to these verses, failure and poverty are not the results of victimization—as is commonly preached in American society! The reason people are stuck in dead-end jobs their whole lives and fail to make progress financially is because of their refusal to make the "knowledge" investment. This lack of planting means a crop failure!

A Better Performance

Advancement through training does not always mean a formal education. For some it may be improving your skills at the job you already hold—reading journals related to your field of expertise or even attending motivational or success seminars.

Regardless of what your profession may be, you can study and better your performance on the job.

The same is true regarding our faith. The Bible tells us: *"Study to show thyself approved unto God, a workman that needeth not to be ashamed, rightly dividing the word of truth"* (2 Timothy 2:15 KJV).

In this verse, Paul was writing to Timothy, a minister-in-training. However, we could apply the same advice to any occupation.

Too Busy?

There are many avenues leading to success, including owning your own business or climbing the corporate ladder. But I assure you, regardless of what area you choose, the more you know about the service, products or industry, the more you will be rewarded financially.

You can't sit like a toad in a hail storm—mesmerized, frozen—and just "confess" your way to abundance. You have to apply yourself.

Many are employed by companies who offer "free" educational opportunities—for college or vocational training courses in their field of work. I am amazed when people miss these chances, saying, "I'm too busy!" Too busy to increase their future earning power?

One man was told he could take off from work (with pay) to further his education. He said, "Pastor, I can't do that. Part-time, it would take three years to get a Masters degree."

I asked him, "How old will you be in three years if you *don't* earn the degree?"

The question wasn't the *time*—he was not prepared to exert the extra effort.

No Excuses

In most cases, to secure your education, you need to be self-motivated.

If you have no one to finance your education, there is always a way! Lack of money should never be a deterrent since it can qualify you to meet the criteria for grants and scholarships. Or, you can enter a branch of the military and receive a top-notch education—while earning a living at the same time.

I have met physicians for whom the government has paid their tuition and expenses, not just during college, but all the way through medical school. The funding was available because doctors are needed in the military.

Of course, it's easier to make education a priority when you're single and young—before you have the duties and obligations of a family and house payments. This is why we encouraged our children to finish their college degrees before marriage—and also why Sue and I waited until I had graduated from college before we were married. We also delayed having children until my doctoral course work was finished.

Please understand, I am not telling anyone what to do; rather, I am suggesting that you pray and, "Think about your options!" Have a plan and work your plan!

An Inheritance

Education is not only "seeding" into yourself, it is an investment in your children. I have seen it demonstrated again and again: the more education you obtain, the more likely your children will have their own aspirations to be educated.

If you have a vision for the future of your children, you will do whatever it takes to put clothes on their backs, shoes on their feet, and give them a head start in life with an excellent education.

Even if you cannot provide houses and wealth, or leave them a dime when you die, if you will invest in your children with a college education, then you will have left them a valuable inheritance.

Check it Out!

Take a personal interest in your child's education—especially at the primary and secondary level. Whether it is public or private, don't simply *trust* the school. Check it out and get involved!

If your child can't read well by the first grade, it's not enough to raise a ruckus, make a change. Move your son or daughter out of the non-productive learning environment and into a quality program.

A child who is unable to read is being handed a life sentence of embarrassment and poverty!

"Wisdom Is Supreme"

Education is not wisdom, but it leads to a place where wise decisions can be made. In fact, we have a much better chance at developing wisdom if we are trained in our profession as opposed to remaining "average." This is why King Solomon says, *"Wisdom is supreme; therefore get wisdom. Though it cost all you have, get understanding"* (Proverbs 4:7).

Unfortunately, I've met those in business and government with degrees from big name schools, yet they have practically no common sense. Wisdom rarely arrives in a total package. Some people have a natural good sense concerning money and economics, but are hopeless with interpersonal relationships. In others, the opposite is true.

When it comes to education versus wisdom, we don't want one or the other—we need both!

The Real Source

How do we build wisdom into our lives? Ideally, it is learned from our mothers and fathers, but there is another source.

The best way I know to add this necessary ingredient is to study the " wisdom literature" of the Word of God—primarily Proverbs and Psalms.

Since there are 31 chapters in Proverbs, the way I built wisdom into my life—especially in my 20s—was to read the chapter in Proverbs which corresponded to the day of the month. I did this daily from the time of my marriage to Sue in 1976 to our departure to serve as missionaries in 1982.

This was invaluable to me during the formative years of our marriage and while I served in my first full-time ministry position in Fort Worth, Texas—also working on my Master of Divinity degree at Texas Christian University. I stayed in Proverbs for *years*, and it planted the wisdom of God into my heart and soul.

No matter how great a job your parents did in child rearing, there are always a few gaps in what your mom and dad taught you. Those deficiencies can be filled with the Word.

If someone were to ask me, "Pastor, would you rather have your formal education or the wisdom of God in your life?" Without hesitation I would answer, "The wisdom of God." But thank God

I have both.

We can *all* add to both our educational and wisdom levels. No one places a limit on us except ourselves!

Keep Investing!

Faith in God and faith in your own abilities is a powerful combination—and paramount to success and prosperity.

Again, the question is not, "Does God believe in you?" He always does! The real question is, "Do you believe in you?"

If the answer is "Yes," for the sake of your future and the building of God's Kingdom, keep investing in your education.

Chapter Eighteen

Conscientious Saving

If you have been reading carefully, you now understand God's plan to bless His people. It is not primarily through "miracle money"—even though there are times of unexplained blessing—but by following the principles of the Word regarding physical labor, faithful tithing, "right living," investing and entering into a covenant relationship with God.

This brings us to step number twelve toward *The God Touch*—conscientious savings.

This challenge requires a plan, diligence, patience and accountability.

A "Faith Goal"

Only a small percent of the population set goals for themselves—including Christians. Personally, I use the term "faith goal" for any objective I establish which requires God's assistance in attaining.

For example, if I set a target of losing ten pounds in the next few weeks, to me this is a goal. However, if I choose the same objective, then ask the Lord every day to assist me in losing those same ten pounds, I consider it a "faith goal." It may also include prayers of agreement with a "prayer partner," positive confession and asking God to help me visualize my ultimate success.

Many Christians have so-called "faith goals," yet they never lift a finger to cause them to become a reality. The phrase, "God helps those who help themselves," has been attributed to everyone from Benjamin Franklin to John Wayne, and it contains a great deal of truth.

In the Bible, you rarely see the Lord doing for people what they can do for themselves. Why? Because it would encourage laziness and trivialize God's awesome power.

On the other hand, if we do for ourselves what He enables us to perform, God will meet us in the process and perform two things:

- First: He will bless the work of our hands.
- Second: He will step in and accomplish whatever we cannot do.

Many continue to look for a "financial miracle," but what we have discovered in our ministry is that prosperity comes from a *combination* of utilizing the practical wisdom of the Word, plus standing in faith for God to answer our prayers and grant the desires of our hearts.

A Principle to Live By

In 1983, when Sue and I returned to the United States from missionary work, all we had was $20,000 profit (after paying a tithe) on the appreciation of our first home. We gave it all to pioneer our ministry.

One morning, five years later—in 1989—I was talking to God concerning my lack of finances, both for our family and the ministry. Of course, at the time I would not admit I was complaining—just "praying!"

While I was on my knees telling the Lord how tired I was of being broke, He said to me, "You don't have any money because you never *save* any money."

In reality, I didn't want to hear anything so practical. No, I wanted a spiritual answer—that an unexpected financial miracle was headed my way.

On that day, God gave me a principle to live by. As I mentioned in an earlier chapter, He told me to save something every seven days, even if it is only five dollars.

The Lord was telling me, "How can I *bless* your money if you never *save* any money?"

"Seed Money"

Everyone knows you can take any number you want, but when you multiply it by zero, you'll still get zero. In other words, *nothing* simply cannot be multiplied.

When the young boy gave Jesus the loaves and the fishes, He "multiplied" them. This miracle would have been impossible unless Jesus was given an amount to start with—regardless of how meager.

Back at my prayer time, the Lord continued, "It is a sin to spend more than you take in."

In obedience to God's clear command, while still tithing to the Lord's work, by 1993, our total savings had increased to $78,000. It was just the beginning of the Lord pouring out His favor on our family and ministry.

I know beyond the shadow of a doubt, the financial increases we have shared with you in this book would never have taken placc without the "seed money" the Lord directed us to save in those early days.

It Multiplied!

A few years later, in 1998, I was in a worship service at church on a Sunday evening. At the conclusion of the meeting, as I was praying, the Lord inspired me with a creative idea concerning my investments.

At that particular time, we had not been receiving our expected returns and it was an issue of concern—so I made it a matter of faith and prayer. I was asking God for practical wisdom in dealing with my savings and investments.

It was as if the Lord told me how to invest in a particular instrument, how to put safeguards (stop losses) in place to protect our capital and how and when to sell that particular investment.

Faithfully, during the duration of 1998, I worked the plan and realized a profit of one million dollars. It had nothing to do with our ministry and took practically no time out of my schedule. Yet it happened!

Please understand, it would have been an impossibility for the Lord to bless me in such a manner if I had not listened, heard and obeyed Him and saved the first $5 fifteen years earlier. There would have been nothing to multiply!

Four Practical Suggestions

Let me offer you three workable ideas regarding how to handle your savings:

Number one: Move as much money into a tax-deferred environment as you possibly can.

The difference between money compounding tax-deferred as opposed to money compounding while taxed is simply phenomenal. Paying taxes on your savings *as you go* diminishes the "power of time" on monetary growth. This is why I recommend placing as much as you possible can in a tax-deferred environment such as an IRA, 401k, 403b or a similar type of savings instrument.

Number two: Have your savings deducted from your paycheck automatically.

I've been doing this for years. Don't even include these monies in your budget. Have it deducted automatically and sent to a tax-deferred savings instrument and "pretend you never saw the money."

If it is transferred in this manner, you will not tinker with it, borrow from it or otherwise play games with the funds.

I am often asked, "What if I am spending every nickel I earn and not saving a percentage of my income? How can I set aside 10% of my earnings?"

We often hear the same type question regarding tithing. New Christians give their lives to Christ, but don't have tithing built into their personal budget. Your 10% to God should be the first money out of your account. And the 10% to yourself—to tax-deferred savings—should be the second money out of your account.

For both the tithe and savings, start where you are and build these amounts into your budget. I recommend you take your next raise and *totally* dedicate the funds to these two expenditures. Even if it takes your next two or three years' worth of raises, apply the increase to tithing and savings. You will never miss the money!

Number three: Make certain your savings—especially retirement monies—are diversified.

Not meaning to be negative toward the firm, I will use the example of AT&T. At one point during the great bull market which ended in March of 2000, AT&T spun off Bell Labs and called it "Lucent." And, of course, there were career employees who had spent twenty or thirty years working for AT&T and quite a bit of their company retirement money was invested in their own stock.

Since AT&T shares had been so stable, their retirement money worked *for* the career people, not against them. When AT&T spun off Bell Labs and created Lucent, Wall Street just "went nuts" over the stock. Lucent shares started at a "split-adjusted" $7.65 in April of 1996, and was bid up to $82.28 in December of 1999.

This seemed too good to be true since it represented a 976% return. But from December, 1999 to October of 2002, the stock dropped to $0.58—a 99% loss. And the drop from where it started in April of 1996 to October of 2002 was 92%. Just think about all those twenty and thirty year veterans of AT&T and Bell Labs who saw their retirement savings drop like a lead ball! And remember: AT&T is not an Enron!

So diversification is important, especially for retirement savings! My point is, when you set those "eggs" aside for retirement, don't put them all in one basket. For the sake of safety, spread them over *several* baskets.

Number four: If you don't control it, you don't own it!

Try to NOT permit your company to control your retirement accounts. Congress has changed the laws and made it too easy for corporations to go through a bankruptcy reorganization and simply walk away from their retirement obligations to their employees. So do everything you can to keep control of your own financial destiny. And if you don't control it and *can't* control it, then my advice would be "Don't count on it!" (See *Time,* October 31, 2005, The Great Retirement Ripoff.")

Forget the Excitement

Some will tell you diversification and the tax-deferred environment are just not that exciting. However, when it comes to retirement savings, we're not wanting stimulating investments—but something sure and steady.

Most stock brokers agree the NASDAQ 100 certainly was volatile from March of 2000 (5,048.62) to October of 2002 (1,210.47). The drop of this major index was 76%. Is *that* "exciting" enough for you—the thrill of a stone dropping from outer space? Is that what you want your retirement account statements to look like?

Too often, we never get the ball rolling enough to where the additional income from savings generates enough to arouse us. Or, sometimes people play games with their investments, where they put $100 into savings, then "borrow" $200 from the same account.

Sure, they intend to put it back, yet never do. And even if they replace the funds, they don't include an extra amount for the interest lost in the meantime. Through their delay or borrowing from themselves, they subvert the power of time and the potency of compound interest as each applies to their savings.

"Richly Blessed"

Time has a way of flying by. I remember telling the Lord, "I love your plan for my life. My only wish is that it could pass by a little slower!"

When your children are small and perhaps "messy and noisy"

and demand 24 hours a day of your time, you sometimes want those years to fly by. Then, one morning you look around and your huggable little children are all grown up—and those baby days are gone forever.

The same thing occurs with money. Solomon said if you delay, or take too many naps, *"...poverty will come on you like a bandit and scarcity like an armed man"* (Proverbs 24:34).

You don't even have to plan for poverty. It just happens "naturally."

Thank God, there is a way to be blessed beyond measure in this life. Scripture tells us, *"A faithful man will be richly blessed, but one eager to get rich will not go unpunished"* (Proverbs 28:20).

I don't know about you, but I would rather be *"...richly blessed..."* than someone who *"...will not go unpunished."*

Restoring the Years

Perhaps you have not been diligent in saving money up to this point in your life. What do you do now? Well, obviously you cannot get into a time machine and erase the years from the calendar. But what you *can* do is start right now—today—to give God the first 10% of all the income that crosses your hands, then "pay yourself" the next 10%—setting it aside in an investment account similar to what we have recommended in this chapter.

Make sure your savings are safely invested, yet growing year by year. If you will do these things, I believe the same God, who says He will "restore the years the locust have eaten," will help you make up for the past.

When you put time on your side, and give God something to bless, nothing will be impossible for you. You will experience the rewarding results of *conscientious saving.*

Chapter Nineteen

Prudent Investing

Some ride on a perpetual merry-go-round. When "plan A" doesn't immediately work, they try plan "B," then rush off to plan "C."

What a frustrating, disheartening lifestyle. How much better to live in the realm where God is literally blessing *all* the work of your hands!

On these pages we have stressed the importance of not only giving God a "tenth," but to set aside an additional 10% every week as a nest egg to grow for your financial future. This is essential as we look at step number thirteen in pursuing *The God Touch*—prudent investing.

Watch the Thorns and Snares

What is to be gained by making the effort to save—only to lose the money by making poor investment decisions?

If we are going to develop ourselves into prudent, careful managers of the funds the Lord has entrusted to us, we need to learn from both our successes and mistakes—and the experience of others.

Pay attention to these words of Solomon: *"A wicked man puts up a bold front, but an upright man gives thought to his ways. There is no wisdom, no insight, no plan that can succeed against the Lord. The horse is made ready for the day of battle, but victory rests with the Lord. A good name is more desirable than great riches; to be esteemed is better than silver or gold. Rich and poor have this in common: The Lord is the Maker of them all. A prudent man sees danger and takes refuge, but the simple keep going and suffer for it. Humility and the fear of the Lord bring wealth and honor and life. In the paths of the wicked lie thorns and snares, but he who guards his soul stays far from them"* (Proverbs 21:29-31;22:1-5).

That's enough food for thought to survive a famine!

Here's the essence of the matter in a nutshell: We need to stay on a clear path, and when danger appears, take refuge.

"The Root"

More than once, I've heard critics attempt to quote scripture and exclaim, "Money is the root of all evil!"

Wait a minute! That's not what the Bible says. Let's read it word for word: *"People who want to get rich fall into temptation and a trap and into many foolish and harmful desires that plunge men into ruin and destruction. For the love of money is a root of all kinds of evil. Some people, eager for money, have wandered from the faith and pierced themselves with many griefs"* (Timothy 6:9-10).

You see, it is not *money*, rather the *"<u>love</u> of money"* which is the root cause of all kinds of evil.

We need to understand that money (in and of itself) is neither good or bad—it is neutral. For example, cash in the hands of a drug dealer is evil, but the same dollars donated to the Red Cross may save lives!

Problems surface when people become hungry and "eager" for money, loving it for the wrong reasons.

No Unmet Needs

It can even happen in the house of God. There are ministers who become so caught up in the "love of money" that they want their flock to give every spare dime to the church—to the point of *abusing* the sheep. Yes, I believe people owe God the tithe and should give offerings as they are led by the Spirit, however, the only way our *entire* membership will grow financially is if they are personally investing and prospering. How else will they be able to leave an inheritance to their children—and their children's children?

When every member obeys the Lord and works His plan, there will never be an unmet need, either in the ministry or in the families who give.

As time moves forward, people are able to present ever-increasing amounts because God is blessing their" barns."

Start With Something!

Don't be tempted to rationalize and say, "When I hit a windfall, I'm going to start saving." This is simply one more excuse.

King Solomon was perhaps the wealthiest man who ever lived,

and we need to listen to his sage advice: *"...he who gathers money little by little makes it grow"* (Proverbs 13:11).

It makes no difference whether you begin with a dollar a day or ten dollars a week, just start with *something!*

As you faithfully and conscientiously set aside 10% into savings of everything you earn, there is going to come a point of "critical mass" where your savings will become an primary income source.

Be Careful of "Brothers"

Let me give you this word of caution. Avoid becoming entangled in business deals with fellow church members—more often than not, it leads to discord and harms the body of Christ.

I am embarrassed to admit that during the early days of our ministry I was "taken in" by two unscrupulous "brothers" in our church. They were constantly pitching money-making opportunities to anyone who would listen.

One day these men invited me to breakfast and "worked me over" regarding investing in a financial instrument they were selling at the time—a real estate trust.

Since I didn't have any liquid cash, they suggested, "Pastor, you could invest in this through your IRA."

My instincts told me this wasn't a good proposition, but in those days I was younger and "dumber." Plus, it was the time of year for me to make my $2,000 contribution to my IRA. So, to get them off my back, I gave them the funds to open an account for me and purchase some shares.

It was problematic from the very beginning. The value of the investment was never in the Wall Street Journal, so I had to call an

800 number to see how the company was doing.

To pour salt in the wound, these two men stopped attending church about a year later. After they moved on, I decided to sell the shares in the real estate trust and merge those funds into my main IRA account—primarily because I was tired of dealing with the firm and hardly ever received a statement.

I took the paperwork to a broker in our city and said, "I made a $2,000 investment and would like to sell. How much is it worth?"

He examined the documents, pressed a few buttons on the calculator, and replied, "You will receive approximately $800 for the shares."

I was stunned. "$800? That's all?"

The broker explained, "You didn't make a $2,000 investment, it was only $1,200."

"Where did the $800 go?" I wanted to know.

"Oh, that was a commission on the deal," he informed me—plus I had lost another $400 on the shares themselves.

I learned an expensive lesson about "investing" with "brothers."

A "Target List"

Years ago, a visitor at our church was quite upset and complained, "I don't like your ushers!"

"Why not?" I asked him.

"Well I'm not sure," he replied. "I was just standing in the lobby, passing my business cards out to everybody coming out of Sunday School and they told me to stop."

"Of course, they did," I told him. "People came here this morning to praise and worship the Lord, not to be confronted by a salesman."

God's house is not the place to come with a "target list" of individuals you want to connect with for business purposes. Whether it's a "multi-level" sales pitch, discount clubs or other "networking" vehicles, the objective is always the same: *using* God's people to make money!

Like yeast working and rising through dough, these people work through church congregations. When they are finished—and have made more than a few members upset—they move down the road to another unsuspecting church. Unfortunately, when they leave, they always try to take their "comrades" with them, including those who *did* sign up for their product, service or network.

In my years of ministry I have discovered an interesting pattern. The same people who won't tithe are the ones who will jump headfirst into "get rich quick" schemes and lose their shirts.

It is my responsibility to protect the people of God from being *used* by other so-called "brothers." I don't knowingly allow such individuals to enter the church and "rip off" members in the name of Christ.

I do not appreciate being *used*—and I'm sure no one else does either!

Double or Nothing?

I advise every young adult to begin investing by setting aside 10% of all of his or her earnings and put that money consistently in the stock market—for an entire lifetime. The strategy works because if the market is down you are buying corporate America at a discount—and when it goes up, so does your net worth.

Historically, this "averaging" has yielded high returns.

Every year, as a person grows older, he should become a little more conservative in his investments. And if someone receives an inheritance at, let's say, 45 years of age, that money should *not* be thrown into the stock market all at once as though it were just 10% of last week's paycheck!

I've met Christians who have a "double or nothing" mentality. Whether you try such an approach in Las Vegas or on Wall Street, you're going to lose your life savings—because amateurs can't go up against professionals.

Beware of the Risk

Keep a close watch on your portfolio.

Sue and I talked with a white haired man who had lost ninety percent of his life savings in the NASDAQ crash. I realize that if someone is twenty years old, and Wall Street enters a cyclical bear market, it doesn't really matter. But I think you would agree an elderly gentleman has no business losing nearly all his savings in investments. He would have to work every day for the rest of his days just to survive.

Some may say, "Well if that man holds on, the NASDAQ and his investments will bounce back."

The last time a United States stock average fell by such a drastic percentage, it took twenty-six years to come back to its old high. Do you feel like waiting that long to break even?

A long Wait!

Successful investors are optimists at heart—believing the market is going *up!* But what if it starts to go south? How long are you going to allow it to slide before taking action?

I may be a fanatic on this, however, I never personally invest in anything I cannot liquidate by the end of the day. There may come a point later in my life when I have other types of holdings, but not now.

Most people don't realize that if an investment goes down just 25% it has to go up 33% for you to break even. And if a stock goes down 50% it needs to go up 100% for you to return to the value you once had. To put it another way, if you had $1,000 and it became $500, you have lost 50%. Yet, if you start with $500 and wanted it to become $1,000, you'd need a 100% return.

No Guarantees

Look at the NASDAQ. From it's peak in March 2000 until the aftermath of the September 11, 2001 tragedy, the NASDAQ dropped 71%. You say, "Don't worry, it will come back." Well, in order for that to happen, it will need to rise 254%. That's a huge amount.

There are no guarantees in investing. What good is a portfolio that is doing well "in comparison to the market" if the entire market is going downhill? This is why I say you also need to understand that when you invest in Wall Street, you're tangling with the big boys and they want your money.

This is why I believe in prudent investing. Let me make these suggestions:

- Avoid investing "on margin."
- Never put money in a church "brother's" business or investment scheme.
- Don't invest capital you can't afford to lose.

- Try to seek higher yields without incurring undue risks.
- Never invest in something you do not, or cannot, understand.

Be careful to always give God the credit for your financial gains, not Wall Street. Why? Because the market is fickle—as the saying goes,"Whatever Wall Street giveth, Wall Street also taketh away."

Diligence And Wisdom

If we want to have plenty at the end of our days, we need to prepare during our productive years.

Diligence and wisdom work hand in hand together. If God gave squirrels enough sense to gather and store food in the good times so they will have plenty to eat in the winter of their life, I think we ought to start paying attention!

Chapter Twenty

Become a Land Owner Instead of a Rent Payer

God is a God of land—and He believes in His people owning property. Look at the Middle East and you will see what I mean. The never-ending dispute between Israel and Palestine is related to God's promise to give His people, Israel, the "Holy Land." Today there is still conflict because both entities consider the territory to be theirs.

If we are going to see the Lord's financial plan for our lives fulfilled, we need to seriously consider *becoming a land owner instead of a rent payer.* It is the fourteenth step to having *The God Touch* upon us.

Consider Your Options

In a conversation with some entrepreneurs in Dallas, I learned they owned their thriving company but were leasing the building in which they operated.

"Have you ever considered constructing your own building?", I asked. "If you put it on a 15-year note, your out-of-pocket money would remain about the same, but at the end of the 15 years you would own the building, debt free."

I explained, "Then, when you retire, the property would produce income for the rest of your lives."

One of the men responded, "We never thought of that!"

"In the Meantime"

Millions operate the same way with their personal housing, saying, "I'll buy the house I *really* want when I can afford it. In the meantime we'll just rent."

The "meantime" often stretches over years and years.

You will never become wealthy writing rent checks to a landowner! All you are doing is paying *his* mortgage payment and giving *him* a profit.

Sue and I decided early in our marriage to own rather than rent and it has been one of the wisest decisions we have ever made. We used the "stair step" approach. Our first home cost $38,950, the second $120,000, the third $275,000—and we later continued to work our way up. Instead of throwing money away, we were building equity. We realized a profit of $22,000 on our first house, broke even on the second and made $150,000 on our third.

I am convinced every young adult—and older people too—can afford to buy rather than rent and should not let another day pass without making this decision.

"The Land I Will Show You"

Property ownership has *always* been important. In fact, real estate was at the center of God's dealing with Abraham. The Lord told him, *"Leave your country, your people and your father's household and go to the land I will show you"* (Genesis 12:1).

With his wife and nephew, Lot, they set out for the land of Canaan. Then, after Lot parted from them and pitched his tent toward Sodom, the Lord appeared to Abraham and said, *"Lift up your eyes from where you are and look north and south, east and west. All the land that you see I will give to you and your offspring forever. I will make your offspring like the dust of the earth, so that if anyone could count the dust, then your offspring could be counted. Go, walk through the length and breadth of the land, for I am giving it to you"* (Genesis 14:14-17).

These verses are sacred to Israelis—and the pivotal reason there has been so much bloodshed between the Jews and the Palestinians to this day. The conflict concerns the question, "Who rightfully owns the land?"

Exert Your Authority

God also told Abraham, *"I am the Lord, who brought you out of Ur of the Chaldeans to give you this land to take possession of it"* (Genesis 15:7).

The Lord first "gave" the land to Abraham, yet this did not mean he could just sit down and vegetate. The former owners still considered the territory theirs, so Abraham had to exert authority—he had to take the land away from them.

When God is ready to transfer property to you, it won't come automatically—you have to exercise your authority.

On that day, the Lord made a covenant with Abraham, saying, *"To your descendants I give this land, from the river of Egypt to the great river, the Euphrates—the land of the Kenites, Kenizzites, Kadmonites, Hittites, Perizzites, Rephaites, Amorites, Canaanites, Girgashites and Jebusites"* (vv.18-20).

Today, if the Palestinians really understood the ramifications of these verses, they would be thanking God for what they *do* have. The Almighty was declaring He was giving Israel the land from the Nile to the Euphrates. If you look at a map of the region, you will understand why the Syrians, Jordanians, Lebanese and Iraqis should be grateful Jews are not literally adhering to Genesis 15—they would own it all!

Why doesn't Israel possess all of this territory today? Because the descendants of Abraham did not exert the leadership required to maintain authority and ownership.

It's a Covenant!

God is a God of dominion—and the earth is *His!* But we are required to "take possession" and occupy what the Lord has given to us.

Later, when Abraham was 99 years old, the Lord appeared to him once more, confirming, *"I will establish my covenant as an everlasting covenant between me and you and your descendants after you for the generations to come, to be your God and the God of your descendants after you. The whole land of Canaan, where you are now an alien, I will give as an everlasting possession to you and your descendants after you; and I will be their God'* (Genesis 17:7-8).

It's Yours!

God fulfills His promises through the work of His people.

Let me illustrate. When you see an engagement ring, the gold was already in the earth—and so was the diamond. Yet someone had to take the time to excavate and "dig it out" from the ground. Then a craftsman used his skills to create the perfect ring setting.

Simply because you desire something, doesn't mean it's just going to be found lying on the road in front of you.

Abraham, and today's Israelites, might have wondered, "How can the Lord give us this land? People are already living there."

Well, the physical property is God's and He can give it to whomever He pleases. There is no point in becoming alarmed because someone is living on what you believe in your heart has been promised to you by the Lord. If God says it's yours—it is!

"Holy Ground"

Later, the Lord gave a similar land-possession message to Moses. While he was tending sheep for his father-in-law, Jethro, the angel of the Lord appeared to him in the form of a burning bush. When he went over to examine and look at this strange sight, God called to him from within the bush, saying, "Moses! Moses!"

And Moses replied, "Here I am."

God continued, *"'Do not come any closer...Take off your sandals, for the place where you are standing is holy ground.' Then he said, 'I am the God of your father, the God of Abraham, the God of Isaac and the God of Jacob.' At this, Moses hid his face, because he was afraid to look at God. The Lord said, 'I have indeed seen the misery of my people in Egypt. I have heard them crying out because of their slave drivers, and I am concerned about their suffering. So I have come down to rescue them from the hand of the Egyptians and to bring them up out of that land into a good and spacious land, a land flowing with milk and honey—the home of the Canaanites, Hittites, Amorites, Perizzites, Hivites and Jebusites'"* (Genesis 17:5-8).

The Earth is "The Lord's"

While the children of Israel were held captive in Egypt by Pharaoh, God sent a series of plagues—including violent storms. This obviously caught Pharaoh's attention. He summoned Moses and exclaimed, *"The Lord is in the right, and I and my people are in the wrong. Pray to the Lord, for we have had enough thunder and hail. I will let you go; you don't have to stay any longer"* (Exodus 9:27-28).

Here was the reply of Moses: *"When I have gone out of the city, I will spread out my hands in prayer to the Lord. The thunder will stop and there will be no more hail, so you may know that the earth is the Lord's"* (v.29).

David echos this same truth as he writes, *"The earth is the Lord's, and everything in it, the world, and all who live in it; for he founded it upon the seas and established it upon the waters"* (Psalm 24:1-2).

I am amazed people can come to church every week, worship God and give financial gifts of love, yet still don't completely understand they are truly His children. And as sons and daughters of the Most High, they have rights—and an inheritance!

If you are a child of the One who owns the whole earth, it also belongs to you—not Pharaoh! The Lord wants you to take possession of this property, enjoy it, and pass it on to your children.

The Lord's Decision

God's desire was for His people to be *"rescued"* from slavery and to be given a land to call their own.

Still, it was up to the children of Israel to *act* on God's prophetic Word. They had to take possession of the territory. The Lord told Moses, *"Speak to the Israelites and say to them: 'When you cross the Jordan into Canaan, drive out all the inhabitants of the land before you. Destroy all their carved images and their cast idols, and demolish all their high places. Take possession of the land and settle in it, for I have given you the land to possess'"* (Numbers 33:51-53).

Scripture reveals God has no issue with giving His people land which our modern legal system would say "belongs to someone else." *"If you carefully observe all these commands I am giving you to follow—to love the Lord your God, to walk in all his ways and to hold fast to him—then the Lord will drive out all these nations before you, and you will dispossess nations larger and stronger than you"* (Deuteronomy 11:22-23).

Moses' successor, Joshua, moved into the place of promise and, with the Lord's help, began conquering the territory. When they came to Jericho, God Himself gave Joshua's men the command to march around the fortified city, and the walls came tumbling down!

Here, the Almighty supernaturally intervened—and accomplished what the people could not do.

Obedience Leads to Ownership

The blessings and favor of God are a reward for right conduct. The Lord admonishes, *"Follow my decrees and be careful to obey my laws, and you will live safely in the land. Then the land will yield its fruit, and you will eat your fill and live there in safety"* (Leviticus 25:18-19).

When we live in obedience to the known will of God, we have every right to believe Him for protection. Living such a lifestyle, we have nothing to fear—because we are following the decrees and statutes of the Father. *"Hear now, O Israel, the decrees and laws I am about to teach you. Follow them so that you may live and may go in and take possession of the land that the Lord, the God of your fathers, is giving you"* (Deuteronomy 4:1).

Why do we follow the commandments of God? So we can "take possession" of His promises. Without obedience, there can be no ownership.

God specifically and repeatedly tells us in His Word how we can live prosperous lives. *"Walk in all the way that the Lord your God has commanded you, so that you may live and prosper and prolong your days in the land that you will possess"* (Deuteronomy 5:33).

Take Charge!

I firmly believe the way today's Christians can fulfill God's command that we "take possession" of the land is to become an owner, not a rent-payer.

Please understand, if you, for whatever reason, are still renting or leasing your home or apartment, don't put yourself down—as long as you have a plan to own property and are diligently working and moving toward such a goal.

Some may protest, "But I live in subsidized housing."

If this is your situation, see it as a stepping stone to eventual ownership. However, if you have a "hand out" mentality and refuse to change, the words on these pages are meaningless.

A Vision for Success

God's will is fulfilled by our action!

Since we live in a "politically correct" generation, some can't grasp the concept of "taking possession." It does not happen by playing games or sabotaging others. Nor can you live in the realm of "I should have done this," or "I could of done that," or "I wish I would have done something else with my life."

All such talk is merely excuse-making and is counter productive. Chasing fantasies will lead you nowhere.

I pray you will develop a *vision* for success and prosperity, so that you can achieve the Lord's dream for your tomorrow. Right now, see yourself enjoying your own home, driving the car you desire and vacationing with your family wherever you please.

This lifestyle of abundance and *independence* means you are *dependent* on no one but yourself and God!

CHAPTER TWENTY-ONE

DO EVERYTHING IN FAITH

If you are excited with the potential of walking through life with *The God Touch*, you must discipline yourself to add this final, fifteenth step—do everything in faith.

I am convinced *all* the effort we exert to secure our success and prosperity, must be done "with faith believing." For example:

- If you are in college, be in *faith* that you can generate the funds to pay the tuition bill.
- Have *faith* you will make good grades—not complaining what a poor student you are!
- If you are going to buy a car, you should make the purchase in faith. Don't mumble under your breath, "Well, I probably won't be able to meet the payments."
- By *faith,* make the decision to move out of your apartment and make a down payment on a home.
- If you're sending out your resume, do so in *faith*.

Even if you're going to have a baby, why not be in faith during the entire nine months? As joyous as a pregnancy is, you're going to have all kinds of new and different things happen to your body. You might experience morning sickness, have trouble sleeping or your feet might even swell.

Why not believe God for a trouble free pregnancy and a healthy, beautiful baby? You are always better off when you bring God into every aspect of life through faith in His Word.

When Sue was pregnant with our children, we prayed over them every day while they were still in her womb.

Anything worthy of your time and attention is also worth getting "in faith" over.

A Moral "Filter"

By operating in this kind of faith and belief daily, you welcome God into your activities as a partner.

Some people don't invite the Lord into everything they're doing because of guilt; their behavior is *wrong* and they know it.

Actually, being in faith over every endeavor serves as a moral "filter." If you cannot sincerely pray and believe God to bless your efforts, it's a good indication you should not be participating in the first place. After all, how can you "get into faith" over drinking tequila?

How can a married man flirt with other women and do it in faith? If you can't bring in God as your partner, stay away!

"I'm Blessed"

A businessman in Dallas is in the habit of calling me "lucky."

However, every time he does so, I quickly correct him, saying, "I'm not lucky. I'm blessed." There is a tremendous difference between the two.

The psalmist didn't write, "The luck of the Lord," rather, *"The **blessing** of the Lord brings wealth, and he adds no trouble to it"* (Proverbs 10:22).

Nearly everyone I know would like to be "blessed," yet many still have a problem with the "wealth" part. Why should we protest if God wishes to shower us with abundance—and doesn't add "trouble"?

Proven Principles

How does the blessing of God come? Is it all God's doing or do we have a part to play? Is prosperity just a matter of following proven, practical principles of wealth creation and financial management? Or, is this *"...blessing of the Lord brings wealth..."* simply a matter of faith, giving and receiving?

After all these years in the ministry and in studying both God's Word and human experience, my wife and I have come to the conclusion that it takes *both*: God's blessing and our effort.

In the process, we need to exercise our faith and apply God's supernatural principles of sowing and reaping.

The "Rewarder"

Many have given up and totally lost sight of the possibility of living a life individually blessed by God, but I am telling you from the Word, "It works!"

Faith is an individual matter. So if you have belief in God's Word, you can enjoy the kind of life where the Almighty confirms

His covenant by giving you the *ability* to produce wealth. We don't have to look for, covet, beg, borrow or steal wealth from our neighbor. By faith in the Word, we can stand on the promise we have been given the ability to produce prosperity!

Another reason we should apply faith to every endeavor is because God is not a "punisher, "but a "rewarder." Scripture tells us, *"But without faith it is impossible to please him: for he that cometh to God must believe that he is, and that he is a rewarder of them that diligently seek him"* (Hebrews 11:6 KJV).

Obey the Rules

Earlier in this book we reviewed the blessings promised by God in Deuteronomy 28, and the list is long, indeed. However, most people gloss over the first verse of the chapter which states the *requirements* for blessings. Here is what it says: *"If you fully obey the Lord your God and carefully follow all his commands..."* (Deuteronomy 28:1).

To receive the results, you must obey the rules!

If you launch out in faith and follow God's commands, everything you put your hand to will have favor. Even *"Your basket and your kneading trough will be blessed"* (Deuteronomy 28:5)!

Years ago, Sue and I began to take this verse literally. We determined the Word was saying our cars would need to be repaired less often, our property would be protected and, yes, our food would last longer in the pantry! To this day, we continually apply faith to every aspect of our lives—materially and spiritually.

Eradicate "Religious" Thinking

World evangelist T. L. Osborn makes this statement: "When people get religion, they stop thinking."

The idea of proving our piety by our poverty is a *religious* concept. However, when you actually study the Bible, you discover the exact opposite. There is hardly a page in the Word which does not talk about blessing, abundance and prosperity. *"See, I set before you today life and prosperity, death and destruction. For I command you today to love the Lord your God, to walk in his ways, and to keep his commands, decrees and laws; then you will live and increase, and the Lord your God will bless you in the land you are entering to possess"* (Deuteronomy 30:15-16).

People are defeated because they do not take God literally at His Word.

If I were to add a sixteenth step to *The God Touch* it would be: Eradicate religious thinking from your mentality! Why? It will cause you to conclude that God wants you to live second-class, miserable lives. This view is *religion*, not Christianity!

Those who believe such mantras are hypocrites. They'll go to church on Sunday and talk about how God wants them poor—then will rush off to work Monday through Friday, even taking on the second shift, to make all the money they can!

Why not be honest and admit we *want* to be successful and prosperous? If the Lord says we are to *"live and increase"* (Deuteronomy 30:16), why can't we accept it as His will?

Live, Don't Merely Exist

As a newly married couple, Sue and I had practically nothing, "living on air." We were in seminary housing in south Fort Worth—it was a sparsely decorated duplex.

One day Sue decided she wanted to go swimming, and talked me into spending a night in a nearby motel where they had a pool.

The one she chose was the only one we could afford—the rooms were just $14.99 a night.

After paying the man at the front desk we went to the room and boy, were we in for a shock! The place was infested with roaches! Not just in the room—when Sue pulled back the sheets the ugly creatures were crawling, not sleeping, even in the bed!

I told my lovely bride, "Honey, I know you want to go swimming, but this isn't living. If this is all we can afford, let's just pass."

So we went to the front desk and asked for our $14.99 back.

Sue and I have discovered over the course of our lives that God wants us to *live*, not merely exist!

Bring Out the Best!

To be prosperous and successful you have to be *willing*, since there is a price to pay. The Bible says, *"If you are willing and obedient, you will eat the best from the land"* (Isaiah 1:19).

That is powerful! If it's the will of God for you to *feast* on the best of the land, it must also be His will for you to *drive* the best of the land—even to *wear* the best of the land.

When Sue and I finally "got it," speaking of this revelation, we determined to live like the children of the King we are. This meant if I could only purchase one-third as many suits, I was going to have the best. And if we could only eat out one-third as often, we were going to enjoy the finest restaurants.

Here is what we discovered: once you get accustomed to excellence, your performance level increases—it brings out the very *best* in you.

Our attitude became, "If God didn't want us to have it, He

should never have told us about it." Why would the Lord tell us *how* to enjoy the best (in Isaiah 1:19) if it were not His will that we indeed *have* the finest? Why would He give us the formula if He did not want us to have the experience?

When you understand the will of God in this matter, you start "going for it"—doing everything in faith, believing that God is helping you succeed!

When I first stepped up to this level and started buying suits I considered to be top quality, I'd only purchase one suit every nine months. That's all I could "afford"—it's where I was at the time.

The Positive Word

Let me say it once more: *Whatever you do regarding your career or your finances, believe that God's hand of blessing is upon you and your every endeavor.*

As you save and invest your money, do so in faith— confessing you have the wisdom of God and the mind of Christ. And if you make a mistake in your investments (which we all do), don't go home and say to your spouse, "How could I be so stupid?" That's also a confession—a negative one.

Speak *only* the positive Word of God.

The Evidence

Success and prosperity are not predicated upon fate or chance.

God gave you the right to set your own course—and the power to choose your future. You are the prophet of your own destiny, not the federal government or the World Monetary Fund. So why not seize that ability—your free will—and use it to your benefit?

When you have *The God Touch* resting on your life, people will know. Oh, they may not understand, yet they will recognize the fact there is a special anointing on you. They will see the evidence! When you *"...keep the commands of the Lord your God and walk in his ways. Then all the peoples on earth will see that you are called by the name of the Lord, and they will fear you"* (Deuteronomy 28:-9-10).

Your Declaration

The only way you will ever "step out of the boat" and walk on the waters of abundance is by applying faith to every word you say and every action you take.

In this book I have presented fifteen steps which will lead to you receiving *The God Touch* on your life. I don't want you to simply read *about* them and say, "Yes, I believe that one is true." I am asking you to confess *each* of these steps—out loud. Do it daily, if necessary, until the words become sealed in your heart and are demonstrated in your behavior.

By faith, declare and decide, with God's help, this is the way you will live:

Step 1: ***"I will give God His tithe."***

Step 2: ***"I will give offerings to the Lord's work as the Holy Spirit leads me."***

Step 3: ***"I will be diligent in my work."***

Step 4: ***"I will be faithful in my marriage."***

Step 5: ***"I will be faithful for the sake of my children."***

Step 6: ***"I will remove toxic people from my life."***

Step 7: ***"I will find a pattern worth emulating—and be true to it."***

Step 8: ***"I will manage my debt."***

Step 9: ***"I will control my spending."***

Step 10: ***"I will confess prosperity."***

Step 11: ***"I will invest in myself through education."***

Step 12: ***"I will be conscientious in my saving."***

Step 13: ***"I will be prudent in my investing."***

Step 14: ***"I will be a land owner instead of a rent payer."***

Step 15: ***"I will do everything in faith."***

I want to thank you for taking this important journey with me. It is my prayer that as you walk in covenant with your Heavenly Father, you will personally experience the eternal blessings of *The God Touch*.

A Final Word

The financial blessings I have written about in this book will not all happen in your life overnight. I'd love to tell you that were so, but it's not. Why? Because the growth of money is a function of time.

As I have mentioned, since the United States is the most prosperous nation on the planet, everyone in this country ought to be a millionaire. It is a land of opportunity. If you can't make it here, you can't make it anywhere!

In Arlington, Texas, I pastor a church filled with a great number of immigrants. I have seen many of these people achieve amazing success, while some native born Americans rest on their laurels and take things for granted.

These immigrants often come from countries where there are few property rights, and little safety or security. When they arrive in America, they go to work—and begin to prosper.

Their spiritual lives are also impressive. Often, they have not been raised in church, yet they come into a ministry such as ours and get involved, making God the primary focus of their lives.

Sue and I have been invited to pray over the homes of many new immigrants in the Dallas/Fort Worth area and it is simply astounding what can be done by someone who finds the Lord and has a positive, "can-do" attitude.

On one such occasion, a wonderful couple from Africa asked us to pray a blessing over their new home. The husband half-way apologized as he said, "Pastor, don't expect too much. It's just our starter home." Yet, when Sue and I arrived, we discovered a beautiful five-bedroom, custom built brick residence! It was quite a starter!

If you are a native-born American, don't complain and cry, "Everything is going wrong. I don't know what I am going to do!"

After reading this book you know *exactly* what action to take. You are going to discover God's prosperity plan and work it! And because the Lord is going to uphold His part of the covenant, I know you are going to succeed.

This is your time to leave the realm of "not enough" and enter the domain of "more than enough." It's a matter of making a commitment to place God and His Word first in your life!

Start living the words of Paul: *"Therefore, I urge you, brothers, in view of God's mercy, to offer your bodies as living sacrifices, holy and pleasing to God—this is your spiritual act of worship. Do not conform any longer to the pattern of this world, but be transformed by the renewing of your mind. Then you will be able to test and approve what God's will is—his good, pleasing and perfect will"* (Romans 12:1, 2)

You can build a new life for yourself in God. I believe, with His help, you can do it!

I invite you to write me and let me know how you are applying these principles—and the affects that they are having on your life.

Dr. Gene Lingerfelt, Pastor
Overcoming Faith Christian Center
6900 US Hwy 287
Arlington, Texas, 76001

A Prayer Of Commitment

Please pray these words with me out loud:

Dear Heavenly Father, I come to You in the precious Name of Jesus, confessing that Jesus is Lord. I believe in my heart You raised Jesus from the dead, for Your Word says in Romans 10:9-10, *"That if you confess with your mouth, 'Jesus is Lord,' and believe in your heart that God raised him from the dead, you will be saved. For it is with your heart that you believe and are justified, and it is with your mouth that you confess and are saved."*

I admit that in times past I have gone my own way and I have paid the price for my sinfulness. I turn from my past, my old way of life, and I ask Jesus to come into my heart as Lord and Savior. Take charge of my life, Lord Jesus. Take away my sin and give me a new future, for your Word says in 2 Corinthians 5:17, *"Therefore, if anyone is in Christ, he is a new creation; the old has gone, the new has come!"*

I commit myself, Lord Jesus, to hear Your Word, read Your Word and be a doer of Your Word. In this, I know my life will change for the better!

Father, I thank You that I am now saved, for Your Word says in Romans 10:13, *"Everyone who calls on the name of the Lord will be saved."*

Thank You for forgiving and receiving me. And, thank You for adopting me into your family, the family of God.

Signed ____

Date ____